INTERNATIONAL
LOWER SECONDARY

Computing

Student's Book

8

Laura Sach

William Collins' dream of knowledge for all began with the publication of his first book in 1819.

A self-educated mill worker, he not only enriched millions of lives, but also founded a flourishing publishing house. Today, staying true to this spirit, Collins books are packed with inspiration, innovation and practical expertise.

They place you at the centre of a world of possibility and give you exactly what you need to explore it.

Collins. Freedom to teach.

Published by Collins

An imprint of HarperCollins*Publishers*
The News Building, 1 London Bridge Street, London,
SE1 9GF, UK

HarperCollins*Publishers*
Macken House, 39/40 Mayor Street Upper, Dublin 1,
D01 C9W8, Ireland

Browse the complete Collins catalogue at
collins.co.uk

10 9 8 7 6 5 4 3 2 1

ISBN 978-0-00-868403-7

British Library Cataloguing-in-Publication Data

A catalogue record for this publication is available from the British Library.

Author: Laura Sach
Publisher: Catherine Martin
Product manager: Saaleh Patel
Project manager: Just Content Ltd
Development editor: Julie Bond
Copy editor: Paul Clowrey
Proofreader: Laura Connell and Tanya Solomons
Cover designer: Gordon McGilp
Cover image: Amparo Barrera, Kneath Associates
Internal designer: Steve Evans, Planet Life Art
Illustrations: Jouve India Ltd
Typesetter: Ken Vail Graphic Design
Production controller: Lyndsey Rogers
Printed and bound by Martins the Printers

This book contains FSC™ certified paper and other controlled sources to ensure responsible forest management.

For more information visit: harpercollins.co.uk/green

Contents

Introduction: How to use this book

The Collins Stage 8 Student's Book and Workbook offer a rich programme of skills development, based on a varied and stimulating set of projects grounded in real-world contexts.

This book series uses six themes relating to computing and digital literacy. These are:

- Our digital world – Providing the tools and insights into safely navigating the digital world around us
- Content creation – Creating content using a variety of software, from office tools to video production
- Create with code – Providing the fundamentals of programming and computational thinking skills
- How computers work – Lifting the lid on the specific technologies that make up a computer system
- Connect the world – Understanding how the world is connected through networks, the internet and the World Wide Web
- The power of data – Collecting, analysing and presenting data linked to real-world activities that create or empower change.

Each chapter is carefully organised to include essential knowledge and skills while working towards the creation of a final project. The final projects are designed to boost creative skills and give you the opportunity to make design decisions and develop projects that matter to you. All units end with a showcase lesson that gives you the opportunity to develop your presenting skills, while gaining valuable feedback on their work.

Stage 8 has eight chapters that relate directly to these six themes, with three chapters dedicated to creating with code.

You will delve into the safe and respectful utilisation of online collaboration tools. Engaging practical activities guide you through the exploration of new machine learning and artificial intelligence concepts. Enhance your software development skills with effective use of flowcharts and prototyping emphasised. Binary representation of data is studied, leading to the collaborative creation of an art installation. Technical aspects of networking, including encryption, are also explored.

Key features of the Student's Book

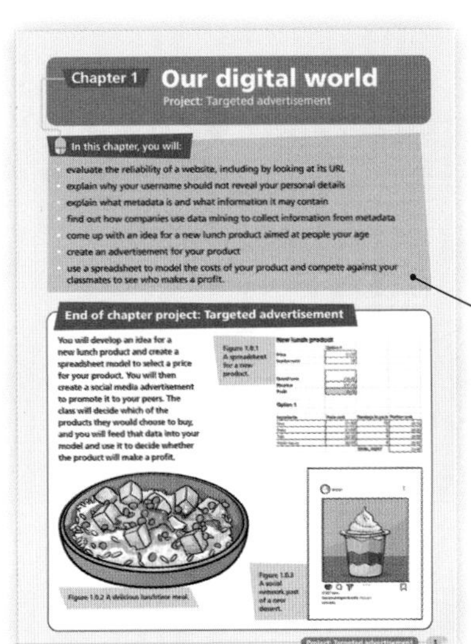

The opening page of each chapter provides an overview of the key activities for that chapter as well as an explanation of the final project, with examples.

Each lesson begins with a helpful reminder of relevant concepts you have already learned about.

Discuss exercises encourage you to develop shared understanding and gain inspiration from your classmates.

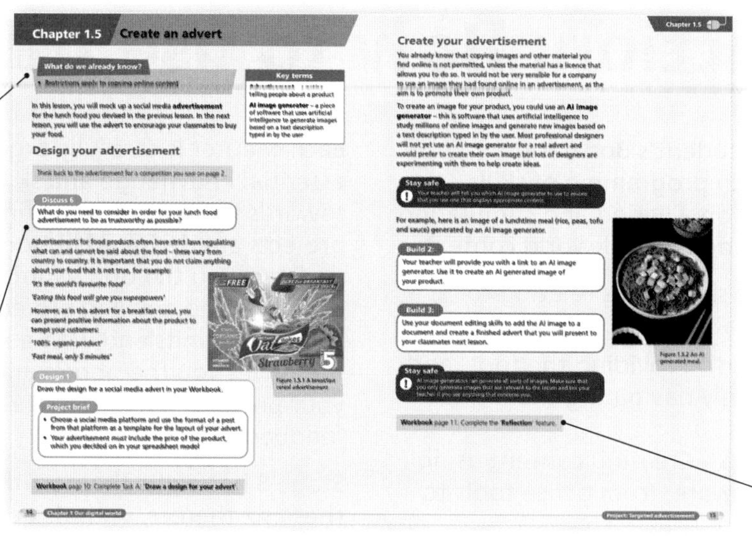

Clear references are provided to tasks to complete in the Workbook.

Helpful tips from the author support you to avoid common problems and make your work the best it can be.

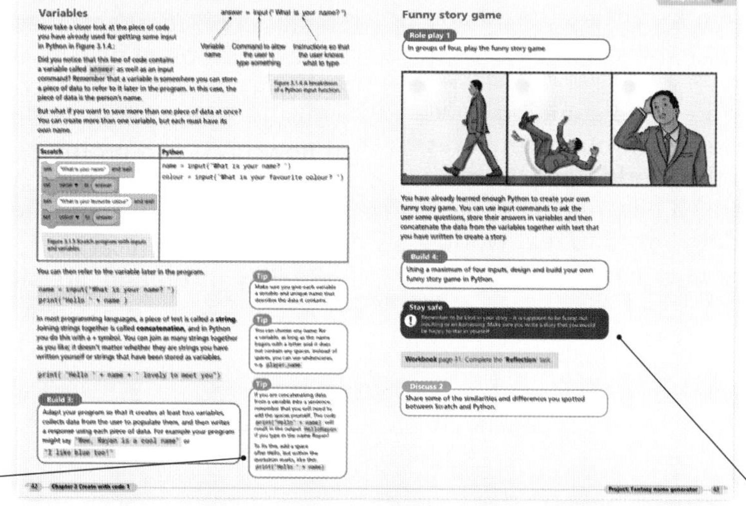

'Stay safe' tips remind you about potential hazards in the digital world.

Showcasing your work develops your communication skills and enables you to receive feedback from others.

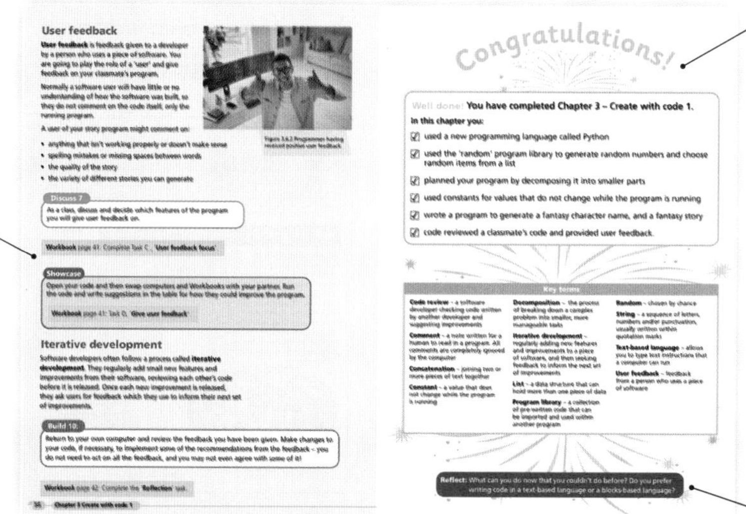

Celebrate what you have achieved and recap your learning at the end of each chapter.

Reflection exercises encourage you to think about what you have learned and achieved and how you feel about your progress.

Chapter 1 Our digital world

Project: Targeted advertisement

In this chapter, you will:

- evaluate the reliability of a website, including by looking at its URL
- explain why your username should not reveal your personal details
- explain what metadata is and what information it may contain
- find out how companies use data mining to collect information from metadata
- come up with an idea for a new lunch product aimed at people your age
- create an advertisement for your product
- use a spreadsheet to model the costs of your product and compete against your classmates to see who makes a profit.

End of chapter project: Targeted advertisement

You will develop an idea for a new lunch product and create a spreadsheet model to select a price for your product. You will then create a social media advertisement to promote it to your peers. The class will decide which of the products they would choose to buy, and you will feed that data into your model and use it to decide whether the product will make a profit.

New lunch product

	Option 1
Price	£1.75
Number sold	10
Overall cost	£14.40
Revenue	£17.50
Profit	£3.10

Option 1

Ingredients	Pack cost	Servings in pack	Portion cost
Rice	£1.90	10	£0.19
Peas	£1.60	8	£0.20
Tofu	£2.20	4	£0.55
Hoisin sauce	£2.00	4	£0.50
		TOTAL COST	£1.44

Figure 1.0.1 A spreadsheet for a new product.

Figure 1.0.2 A delicious lunchtime meal.

Figure 1.0.3 A social network post of a new dessert.

Chapter 1.1 Evaluating online information

What do we already know?

- How to check whether a website is secure

Key terms

Uniform Resource Locator (URL) – a unique address which specifies the location of a website

A tempting advertisement

Discuss 1

A friend has sent you a link to this website. Would you enter the competition? Give reasons for your choice.

https://youwincar.hyz

WIN this amazing car

You could win the car of your dreams! Enter your email below to play!!!

Email:

I want to win

You have 00:01:36 hours until the draw - BE QUICK!

Figure 1.1.1 An online competition advertisement.

In this lesson you will learn a variety of methods to help you to evaluate whether the information you see online is reliable.

What can you tell from the URL?

Every piece of content accessed via the web has a **Uniform Resource Locator (URL)**, which is a unique address for that document, image or other type of file. You can find out a lot of information about a webpage without even visiting it, just by looking at its URL. Here is the URL for the publisher of this book in Figure 1.1.2.

This webpage sends its information via HTTPS – the 'S' stands for 'secure'. When you send or receive information from a website, if the protocol displayed is 'https', the information is encrypted so that no one else can read it. Some webpages use a less secure protocol called HTTP to send and receive data, which means that data you type in, such as credit card details, could potentially be read by other people.

The domain name of the website is harpercollins.com – this name was chosen and paid for by the company. Each domain name is unique, so once a domain name has been bought, no other website can use the same name.

Tip

Be careful about following links to websites you are not familiar with, especially if they are presented to you unexpectedly, for example in an unsolicited email or a pop-up.

The method the website uses to send and receive information

https://www.harpercollins.com

The domain name

The top level domain (TLD)

Figure 1.1.2 A breakdown of the Harper Collins domain.

Stay safe

Sometimes scam websites are created to impersonate legitimate websites. Scammers will often purchase a very similar domain name, or one with a misspelling, hoping that users will not notice. Always check the spelling of the domain name when you visit a website.

The .com part of the URL is called the top-level domain, or TLD for short. A .com domain tells you that this is a website for a company (although individuals can also buy domain names ending in .com). There are hundreds of other TLDs, for example, .org is used worldwide by charities and non-profit organisations. Each country also has its own TLD, for example: .ae for the United Arab Emirates, .tz for Tanzania, and .in for India. Individual countries have different rules about who can use their top-level domain.

Figure 1.1.3 Examples of web domains.

Workbook page 1: Complete Task A, '**Evaluate the URL**'.

Is the information reliable?

If you are looking at a social media post or a video, looking at the URL is not enough to be able to determine whether the information you are looking at is reliable because the protocol and TLD will have been set by the social network or video hosting platform.

Instead, here are some questions you could ask yourself to help make an accurate judgement:

- What is the purpose of the information?
- How well written is it?
- (If the information is an advert) If you search for this product using a search engine, what do you find?
- Is the social media account verified?
- Have you heard of the company, organisation or individual?

Workbook page 2: Complete Task B, '**Mind map**'.

Investigate 1

Look at the social media post worksheet provided by your teacher and evaluate how reliable you think the post is. Annotate your thoughts on the worksheet.

Workbook page 3: Complete the '**Reflection**' task.

Chapter 1.2 Usernames and metadata

What do we already know?

- The consequences of online activity within a digital footprint

Key terms

Cookie – a small amount of data stored on your computer by a website

Metadata – 'data about data', for example who created the data, when it was created, and what device it was created on

Usernames

When you sign up for a website, create an email address or use any online service that requires you to log in, you will be asked to create a username and password. Your password should be known only by you, but the username you choose is often publicly viewable by anyone.

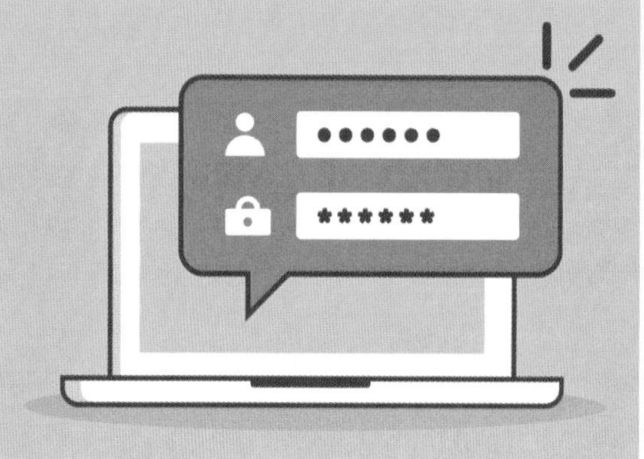

Discuss 2

What information might a username leak about the user's identity?

ILoveHorses0808

nazzyyy_2010

jellybean123

LondonBoy

TheRealAjayB

Figure 1.2.1 A selection of usernames.

Workbook page 4: Complete Task A, '**Why choose an anonymous username?**'.

Discuss 3

Join up in a group with other students and compare your answers. Each person should read their list in turn, and the other members of the group should:

- agree, if they wrote the same point
- challenge, if they think that the answer is incorrect
- note it down, if they agree with the point but did not think of it

What is metadata?

Information about you is not just leaked by means of your username. When you browse the web, you leave a trail of invisible information behind you. Everything you do generates data – the sites you visit, the links you click on, the words you type and the items you put in your shopping basket in an online store – even if you don't buy them!

Metadata literally means 'data about data'; for example, who created the data, when it was created, and what device it was created on. Every action you take online provides some form of metadata which describes the context of what you were doing.

Omari visited an online shopping website. This is some of the metadata that was collected about his visit.

The device Omari used to browse the website; for example, whether it was a desktop, laptop, tablet or mobile phone. The brand and model of the device may also be collected.

Which pages on the website Omari visited and how long he stayed on each page.

The date and time he visited the website.

Workbook page 4: Complete Task B, '**What metadata is recorded?**'.

The items he searched for using the website's search function and how he referred to them. For example, the search terms 'trousers', 'pants', 'joggers' and 'tracksuit bottoms' might all lead to the same product.

Cookies

A **cookie** is a small amount of data stored on your computer by a website. In most European Union countries, websites must by law ask for permission to store cookies, but laws vary in other countries, and websites can store cookies without your knowledge or consent.

Cookies store small pieces of information about the user. Here is an example of a cookie stored on a user's computer in the United Kingdom, by an online shopping website.

Cookie Value ☐ Show URL-decoded

{"countryISO":"GB","currencyCode":"GBP","cultureCode":"en-GB"}

You can see from the cookie that the website has found out that the user lives in 'GB' (Great Britain), the user pays in 'GBP' (British Pounds) and speaks 'en-GB' which is the code for British English. Saving this data in a cookie means that next time the user visits the website, they will automatically be shown the information in their preferred language and currency.

Investigate 2

You can inspect the data stored in cookies which are saved on your device.

If you are using Google Chrome, right click/control click on any webpage, select 'Inspect', click on the 'Application' tab and select 'Cookies'.

Can you find any interesting data being stored in cookies?

Workbook page 5: Complete Task C, '**Data from cookies**'.

Workbook page 5: Complete the '**Reflection**' task.

Chapter 1.3 Data mining

What do we already know?

- Metadata is collected when you browse the web and can include the date and time of your visit, what you clicked on and search terms you typed
- How to use basic spreadsheet functionality and formulae, including AVERAGE

Key terms

Data mining – analysing large amounts of data to find patterns and trends

IP address – an address allocated to you by your internet service provider, which reveals your rough geographical location. An IP address looks like a set of four numbers separated with a dot, for example 172.217.22.14

Why collect metadata?

Metadata is often collected for technical purposes. When you visit a website, the site logs your public **IP address**, which is allocated to you by your internet service provider. Your IP address can be used to find out your rough geographical location – a country and perhaps a city where you live.

Here are some technical reasons why metadata is useful:

Tip

You can find out your public IP address by typing 'what is my IP address' into the Google search engine.

Figure 1.3.1 It is useful for a web developer to know which device someone is using to view a webpage, so that they can present either the desktop or mobile version of the website.

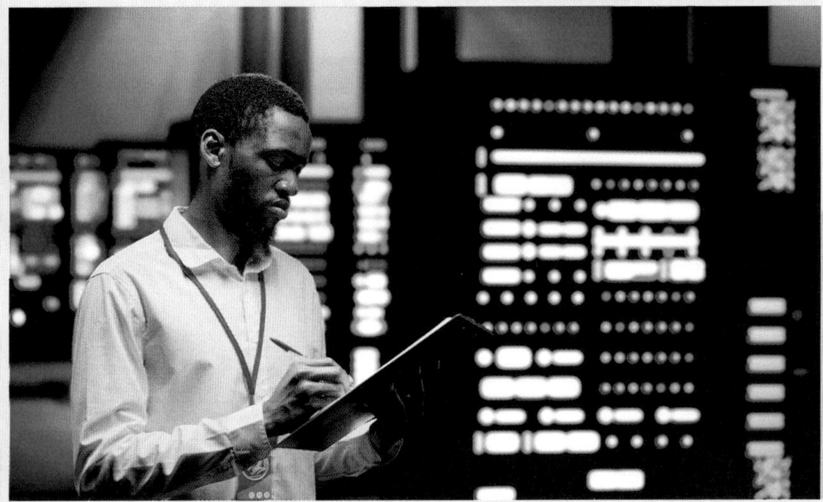

Figure 1.3.2 The time and date of a user's visit is logged so that programmers can analyse when a website will experience peak traffic. For example, a ticket booking website will experience a very high number of simultaneous visits when tickets to a popular event are released.

Figure 1.3.3 Your IP address is logged by community websites so that, if you misbehave, you can be blocked from using the website by IP address.

How do companies use metadata?

Companies started to notice in the 1990s that they could use the data being collected incidentally by their computer systems to discover patterns and trends about their customers and their buying habits. Analysing large amounts of data in this way is known as **data mining**.

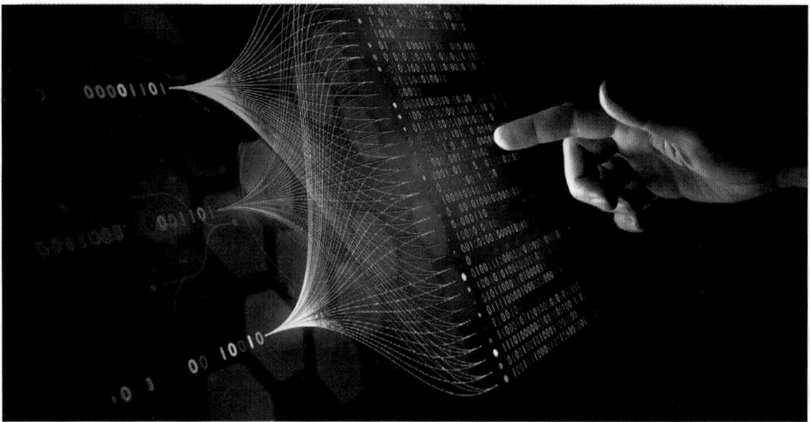

Discuss 4

Think about each of the following pieces of metadata. Why do you think a *company* would want to know this data about a user browsing on its website?

- Device used to visit the page
- Date and time of user visit(s)
- Which pages were visited
- Words typed into the website's search feature
- User's IP address

Record your answers in your Workbook.

Workbook page 6: Complete Task A, '**Why is metadata useful?**'.

Data mining

When companies analyse data, they often have sophisticated programs and statistical tools to help them. You are going to try to do some data mining using a spreadsheet. This will involve spreadsheet functions that you have already learned about.

One very useful tool a spreadsheet has is the ability to quickly sort data. Here is how to do this using Google Sheets.

To sort data:

- Select all your data (including the column headers) by clicking and dragging to highlight it. It is important to select *all* of the rows containing data, not just the ones you want to sort.
- Select Data > Sort range > Advanced sorting options

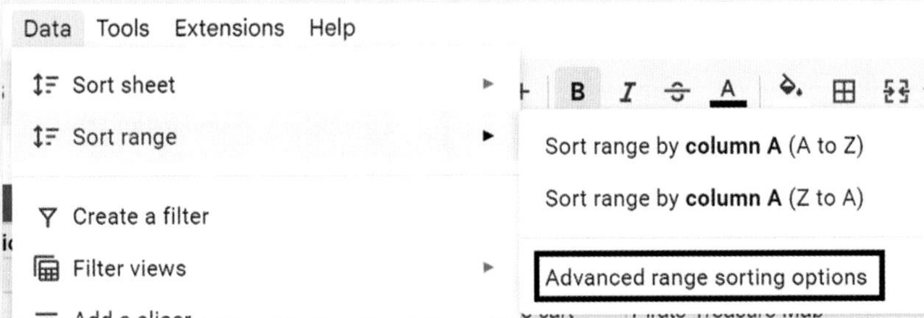

Figure 1.3.4 Sorting menu.

- Tick 'Data has header row' and then select the column you would like to sort by.

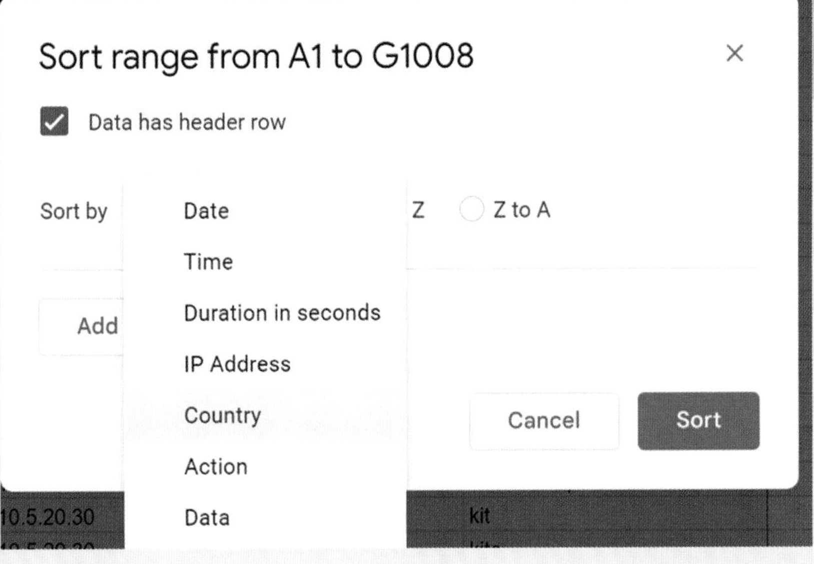

Figure 1.3.5 Sorting column selection.

- It is possible to sort by more than one column. Add the first column to sort by, then click the 'Add another sort column' button and add another column. The data will be sorted by the column you selected first, and then, within that, will be sorted by the second column.

You will also need to use the **AVERAGE()** formula you have already learned in the previous stage. This formula can be used to find the mean average of a range of cells.

	A	B
1	1	
2	5	
3	2	
4	? =average(A1:A3)	
5		

Figure 1.3.6 The AVERAGE function.

Investigate 3

Try data mining using metadata from a fictional online shop which sells products for teenagers. Your teacher will provide you with the data. Fill in the answers to the questions in Workbook page 6: Task B, 'Interrogate the data'.

Tip

It is important to understand that the scale of the data you have worked with is nowhere near as large as the amount of data that would be collected and analysed by a real company.

Stay safe

Talk to your teacher or another adult if you are concerned about anything you have learned about.

Workbook page 7: Complete the '**Reflection**' task.

Chapter 1.4 Models

What do we already know?

- Companies use data to help them to make decisions
- How to use spreadsheet formulae, including SUM and AVERAGE
- How to use conditional formatting to change the colour of cells depending on their value
- How to format cells in a spreadsheet
- Mathematics: how to round a number to two decimal places

Key terms

Cost – the amount that has to be spent, e.g. on ingredients for a product

Model – a simulation of a real-life system on a computer

Profit – revenue minus any costs

Revenue – the amount of income generated from selling a product

What is a model?

Modern companies make use of data about their customers to help them to make decisions about what products will be successful and who to advertise them to. A **model** is a simulation of a real-life system on a computer.

Many people now have smart monitors, or meters, in their homes that monitor how much electricity or gas they use and then send this data directly to the energy company. The company adds all of the data they collect to a model and uses the model to predict when demand will be highest, and sets prices accordingly.

Figure 1.4.1 An energy smart meter.

Large taxi companies use a model to understand where each car is, and to show the closest options to anyone who is looking for a ride. They can also adjust their prices if there is a high demand in a particular area; for example, if lots of people want to be picked up at the end of a particular event.

Figure 1.4.2 A woman searching for taxis using her location

Some models are used for safety and product quality testing. For example, engineers use a computer to simulate components they have designed and use the model to 'stress test' how the component will react; for example, to check that the component will not break if a lot of force is exerted on it. This is much faster and cheaper than testing an actual component and the results are easier to measure than performing the test with real materials.

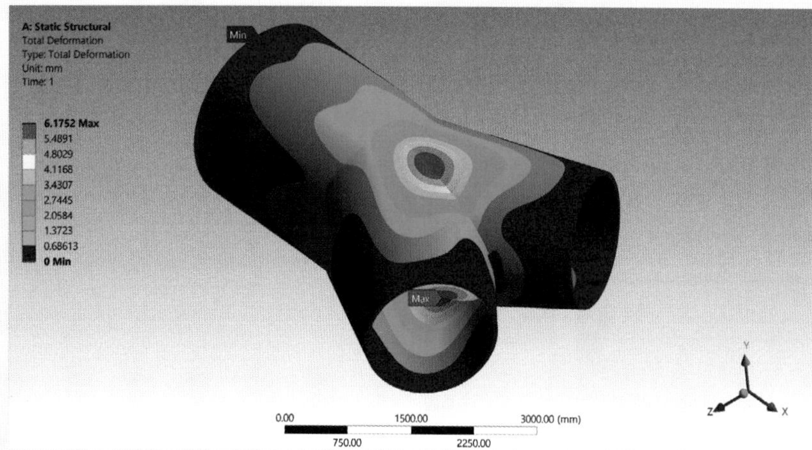

Figure 1.4.3 3D model virtual testing.

Data requirements

All models require data to be able to simulate the real-life situation, and rules to determine how the model behaves.

Discuss 5

Your teacher will allocate you one of the models described above. With your group members, discuss what data you think would be required for this model.

New food product

Project brief

You are going to create a model to help you to devise a lunch product to sell, aimed at people your age.

You will:

- think of an idea for a new product, which might be a lunchtime meal, a special dessert or an exciting drink
- research the cost of the ingredients of your product
- calculate the total cost to make the product
- decide on the sale price of your product
- create a model that tells you how much profit or loss you will make depending on how many products you sell
- use formulae in your model whenever you do a calculation.

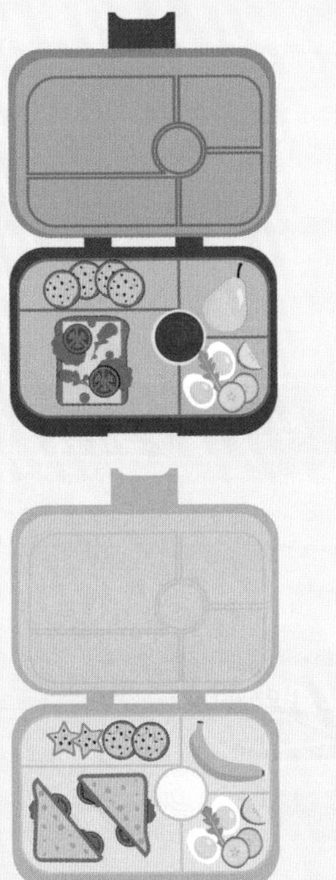

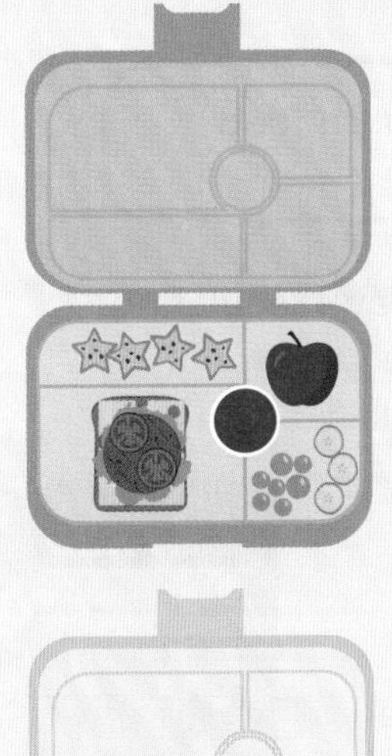

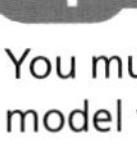

Tip

You must use formulae in your model whenever you do a calculation, otherwise you will not be able to change the values to model different scenarios.

Figure 1.4.4 School lunch boxes from around the world.

Build 1:

Decide on a product. Your teacher will give you the starter spreadsheet. Follow the checklist in Workbook page 8: Task A, 'New lunch product' to create your model.

In the next lesson, you will create a social media advertisement for your product and use your model to determine whether or not you made a profit.

Workbook page 9: Complete the '**Reflection**' task.

Chapter 1.5 Create an advert

What do we already know?

- Restrictions apply to copying online content

Key terms

Advertisement – a notice telling people about a product

AI image generator – a piece of software that uses artificial intelligence to generate images based on a text description typed in by the user

In this lesson, you will mock up a social media **advertisement** for the lunch food you devised in the previous lesson. In the next lesson, you will use the advert to encourage your classmates to buy your food.

Design your advertisement

Think back to the advertisement for a competition you saw on page 2.

Discuss 6

What do you need to consider in order for your lunch food advertisement to be as trustworthy as possible?

Advertisements for food products often have strict laws regulating what can and cannot be said about the food – these vary from country to country. It is important that you do not claim anything about your food that is not true, for example:

'It's the world's favourite food'

'Eating this food will give you superpowers'

However, as in this advert for a breakfast cereal, you *can* present positive information about the product to tempt your customers:

'100% organic product'

'Fast meal, only 5 minutes'

Figure 1.5.1 A breakfast cereal advertisement.

Design 1

Draw the design for a social media advert in your Workbook.

Project brief

- Choose a social media platform and use the format of a post from that platform as a template for the layout of your advert.
- Your advertisement *must* include the price of the product, which you decided on in your spreadsheet model

Workbook page 10: Complete Task A: '**Draw a design for your advert**'.

Create your advertisement

You already know that copying images and other material you find online is not permitted, unless the material has a licence that allows you to do so. It would not be very sensible for a company to use an image they had found online in an advertisement, as the aim is to promote their own product.

To create an image for your product, you could use an **AI image generator** – this is software that uses artificial intelligence to study millions of online images and generate new images based on a text description typed in by the user. Most professional designers will not yet use an AI image generator for a real advert and would prefer to create their own image but lots of designers are experimenting with them to help create ideas.

Stay safe

Your teacher will tell you which AI image generator to use to ensure that you use one that displays appropriate content.

For example, here is an image of a lunchtime meal (rice, peas, tofu and sauce) generated by an AI image generator.

Figure 1.5.2 An AI generated meal.

Build 2:

Your teacher will provide you with a link to an AI image generator. Use it to create an AI generated image of your product.

Build 3:

Use your document editing skills to add the AI image to a document and create a finished advert that you will present to your classmates next lesson.

Stay safe

AI image generators can generate all sorts of images. Make sure that you only generate images that are relevant to the lesson and tell your teacher if you see anything that concerns you.

Workbook page 11: Complete the '**Reflection**' feature.

Chapter 1.6 'What if' analysis

What do we already know?

- Mathematics: To calculate a value after a percentage increase, you can multiply the original value by a number larger than 1. For example, multiplying by 1.1 will increase a value by 10%

Key terms

'What if' scenario – a simulation involving a set of criteria being applied to a model, so that the result can be observed

Run the simulation

In a previous lesson, you created a spreadsheet to model the costs of the ingredients involved in creating your new lunch product idea. In this lesson, you will use your advert to advertise your product to the class and run a simulation to see how many people would choose to buy it.

Role play 1

Your teacher will give you the instructions for this role play task. All of the adverts for the different lunch products will be displayed and you will be able to choose which products to 'buy'. Your teacher will give you the results.

Figure 1.6.1 Students in a roleplay activity.

Build 4:

Input the numbers given to you by your teacher into your model and see how much profit you have made in round 1.

'What if' scenarios

The main reason for building a model is so that you can use the model to change different data values and ask questions – this is called a **'what if' scenario**.

Here are some questions you could ask about the real-life models you saw on pages 11 and 12:

Figure 1.6.2 What if there is unexpected cold weather?

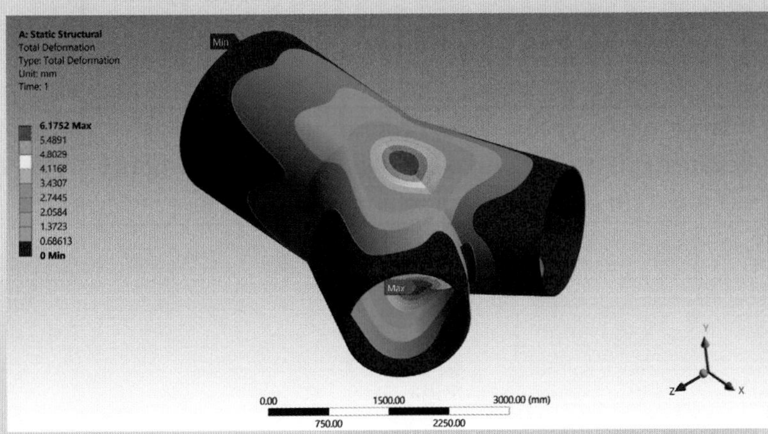

Figure 1.6.3 What if a large volume of water flows through the pipe at once?

You can use the model you have built to ask 'what if' questions.

Here is a model of a student's meal choice, from a student in the UK. The total cost of their meal is £1.44, and they are selling one portion for £1.75. If they sell 10 meals, they will make £3.10 in profit.

New lunch product

	Option 1
Price	£1.75
Number sold	10
Overall cost	£14.40
Revenue	£17.50
Profit	£3.10

Option 1

Ingredients	Pack cost	Servings in pack	Portion cost
Rice	£1.90	10	£0.19
Peas	£1.60	8	£0.20
Tofu	£2.20	4	£0.55
Hoisin sauce	£2.00	4	£0.50
		TOTAL COST	£1.44

Figure 1.6.4 Spreadsheet model showing potential profit.

Then they apply a 'what if' question to their model:

What if?	The price of all ingredients increases by 25%.
What did you change?	I multiplied the portion cost of all ingredients by 1.25.
What was the result of this change if you still sell 10 products?	Previously I made £3.10 profit but now I am making a £0.50 loss.
How many products do you now need to sell to cover your costs?	If the price stays the same, I cannot make a profit because it is now more expensive to make my product (£1.80) than the price I am selling it for (£1.75).

New lunch product

	Option 1
Price	£1.75
Number sold	10
Overall cost	£18.00
Revenue	£17.50
Profit	-£0.50

Option 1

Ingredients	Pack cost	Servings in pack	Portion cost
Rice	£1.90	10	£0.24
Peas	£1.60	8	£0.25
Tofu	£2.20	4	£0.69
Hoisin sauce	£2.00	4	£0.63
		TOTAL COST	£1.80

Figure 1.6.5 Spreadsheet model following 'what if' changes.

Workbook page 12: Complete Task A, '**What if scenarios**'.

Build 5:

Devise a new 'what if' scenario that could happen in your model. Write your scenario on a piece of paper and hand it to your teacher.

Build 6:

Apply the scenario you have been given to your model. You are then allowed to make a *maximum* of two changes to your advert as a result of this scenario. For example, you may want to change the price, swap an ingredient, or make a change to your advert.

Role play 2

You will re-run the same role-play exercise, but with the new advertisements. Your teacher will provide you with the results to input into your model.

Your teacher will collate the results and announce which lunch product idea made the most profit.

Workbook page 13: Complete the '**Reflection**' task.

Well done! You have completed Chapter 1, 'Our digital world'.

In this chapter you:

- ☑ evaluated the reliability of a website, including by looking at its URL
- ☑ learned why your username should not reveal your personal details
- ☑ found out about metadata, and how companies use it to discover information about their customers
- ☑ devised an idea for a new lunch product
- ☑ created a social media advertisement for your product
- ☑ used a spreadsheet to model the cost of your product
- ☑ competed against your classmates to see whose product was the most profitable.

Key terms

Advertisement – a notice telling people about a product

AI image generator – a piece of software which uses artificial intelligence to generate images based on a text description typed in by the user

Cookie – a small amount of data stored on your computer by a website

Data mining – analysing large amounts of data to find patterns and trends

IP address – an address allocated to you by your internet service provider, which reveals your rough geographical location. An IP address looks like a set of four numbers separated with a dot, for example 172.217.22.14

Metadata – 'data about data', for example who created the data, when it was created, and what device it was created on

Model – a simulation of a real-life system on a computer

Uniform Resource Locator (URL) – a unique address which specifies the location of a website

'What if' scenario – a simulation involving a set of criteria being applied to a model, so that the result can be observed

Reflect: What can you do now that you couldn't do before?

Chapter 2 Content creation

Project: Virtual tour

In this chapter, you will:

- describe when it is appropriate to use emojis, gifs and memes
- design a document template and understand its benefits
- practise your typing
- improve your skills when using a search engine
- use sound, video, images and text to create a virtual tour
- learn about augmented reality and when it can be used.

End of chapter project: Virtual tour

In this chapter, you will work with a partner to design and create a virtual tour of a place that is familiar to you. This might be your school or an interesting place near where you live such as a landmark or a museum. People will be able to take your virtual tour to find out more about the place as if they were visiting it in person.

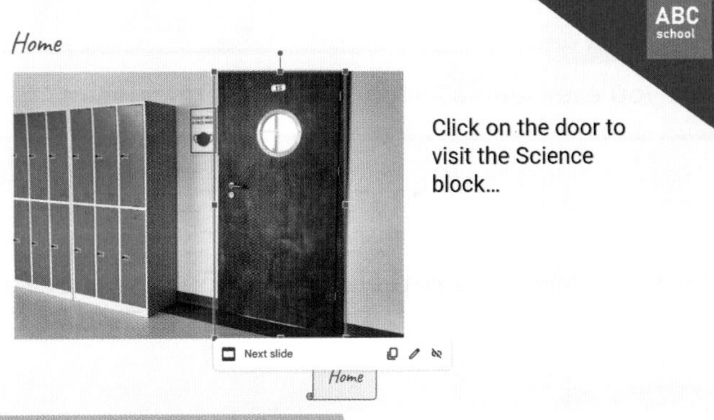

Figure 2.0.1 A classroom door.

Figure 2.0.2 A local lighting landmark.

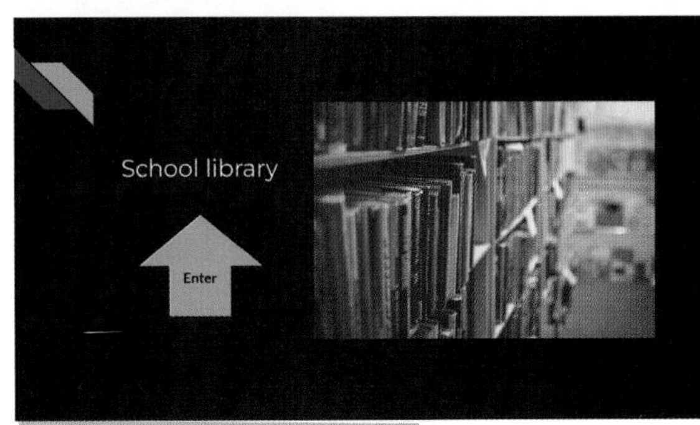

Figure 2.0.3 A library corridor.

What is a virtual tour?

If you want to see inside a particular place, but you cannot physically go there, you might choose to do a **virtual tour**. A virtual tour is a computer simulation of a location which lets you move around to look at different things. The tour probably involves images and text but may also involve sound and video.

Figure 2.1.2 A virtual tour around a house.

Key terms

Audience – the people who will look at the work you produce

Emoji – a small icon used in text to express an emotion or represent an item

GIF – an image format which allows animation

Meme – a familiar image, often accompanied with text, which is shared and reused on the internet

Virtual tour – a simulation of being at a particular location, involving multimedia such as images, text and perhaps also sound and video

Discuss 1

Have you ever seen a virtual tour? Where was this?

Investigate 1

Find an example of a virtual tour and look at the features.

Stay safe

If your teacher asks you to search for a virtual tour, you should be able to find one that can be accessed without downloading any software. If you see anything that makes you feel uncomfortable, tell your teacher.

Workbook page 15: Complete Task A, '**Features of a virtual tour**'.

Who might use a virtual tour?

A virtual tour is useful in situations where it is impossible to visit the place in person.

You might choose to do a virtual tour because:

- the place might be too expensive or take too long to get to
- you may be unable to travel, for example due to illness
- you may want to familiarise yourself with a place you are intending to visit before you get there

Virtual tours are often used to allow people to look around a house that is for sale. A virtual tour means that the occupants of the house are not constantly disrupted by visitors.

Figure 2.1.2 A virtual estate agent tour.

Some virtual tours are of places that it is either very dangerous or impossible to go. For example, a virtual tour of a shipwreck far below the ocean, or a simulation of what it is like inside the human body.

Know your audience

To make a virtual tour, you will need to think about the types of people who will use it. These people are called your **audience**. You may not realise it, but when you communicate, you are constantly thinking about your audience. For example, you might communicate very differently with a friend compared with a teacher or elderly relative.

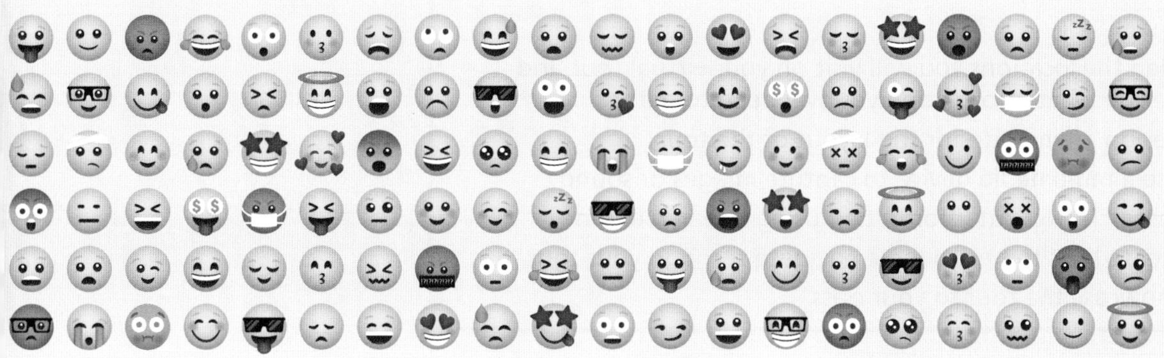

Figure 2.1.2 Examples of emojis.

Emojis are small icons used in text to express an emotion or represent an item. They are often used as a short way of writing something, and emerged as a result of typing being more difficult on older computers and mobile phones, which used text-based messaging.

Figure 2.1.3 A typical meme image.

Memes are familiar images, often accompanied with text, which are shared and reused on the internet. They often represent a feeling or a situation.

GIFs are similar to memes in their content, but the name 'GIF' actually refers to the image file format name, which allows the image to be animated, like a very short movie clip. For example, you might send someone a GIF of confetti to say congratulations on their birthday.

Workbook page 15: Complete Task B, '**When is it appropriate?**'.

Plan your tour

Project brief

In this chapter, you will work with a partner to create a virtual tour of a place that you know well. This might be your school, or it could be an interesting place in your local area, such as a museum or a landmark.

You will:

- plan the locations you will visit on your virtual tour and decide what information you will need to gather
- design a template for the layout of the tour
- use a multimedia device to capture images or sound
- research relevant information using a search engine
- create links to help people navigate through your tour
- showcase the tour to your class

Workbook page 16: Complete Task C, '**Plan your virtual tour**'.

Workbook page 17: Complete the '**Reflection**' task.

Chapter 2.2 Document templates

What do we already know?

- How to use presentation software
- The audience you have chosen for your virtual tour

Key terms

Template – a pre-designed format for a document

Discuss 2

What is a template?

What is a template?

When you create a document, you don't have to start from a blank page. Instead, you could use a **template** which is a pre-designed format for the document. A template could include:

- a colour scheme
- fonts
- text sizes for different parts of the document
- spaces for images
- shapes or patterns that are repeated throughout the document
- specific pieces of information that should be on every document, for example a company logo, or a social media handle.

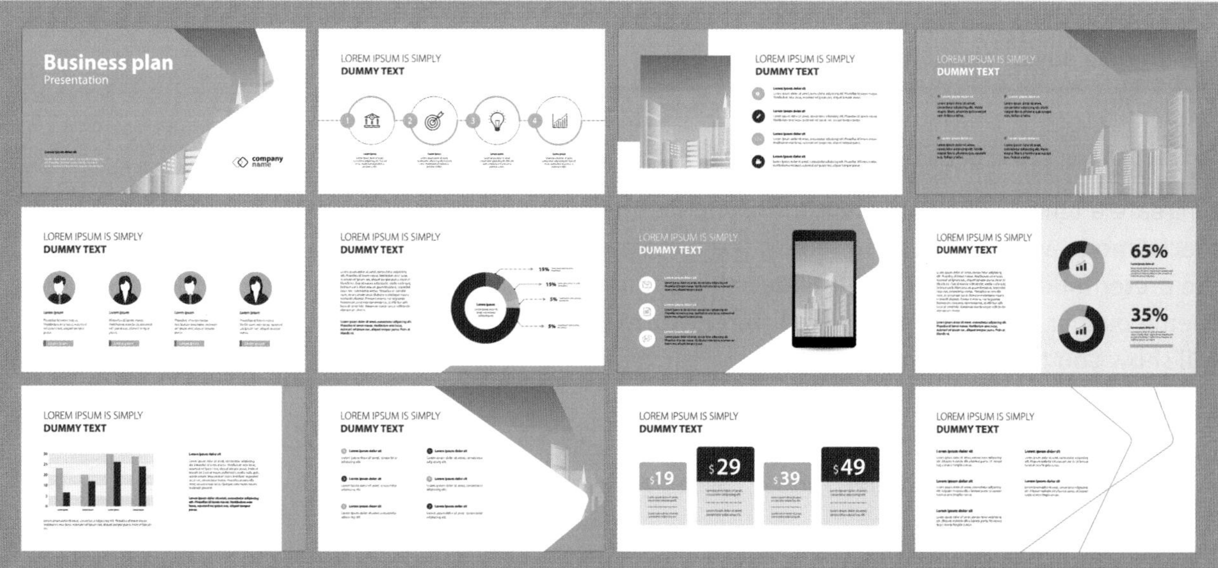

Figure 2.2.1 A document template for a presentation.

Consider the audience

During the previous lesson, you saw that using emojis, memes and GIFs were appropriate in some situations and not in others. The design of a template is important because it needs to be appropriate for your audience.

Here is an example of a document template. It is a template for a leaflet.

Figure 2.2.2 A document template for a printed document.

Discuss 3

Would this template be appropriate for each of the following purposes? Why, or why not? Think about the features of the template listed on the previous page to help you answer.

- To advertise a nursery
- To promote a charity which helps starving children
- To give advice about healthy eating

Using a presentation template

To create a template for a presentation, you first need to enter a special mode, which allows you to edit the template rather than the presentation itself. In Google Slides, this is found under View > Theme builder, but if you are using different software your teacher will show you the correct menu option.

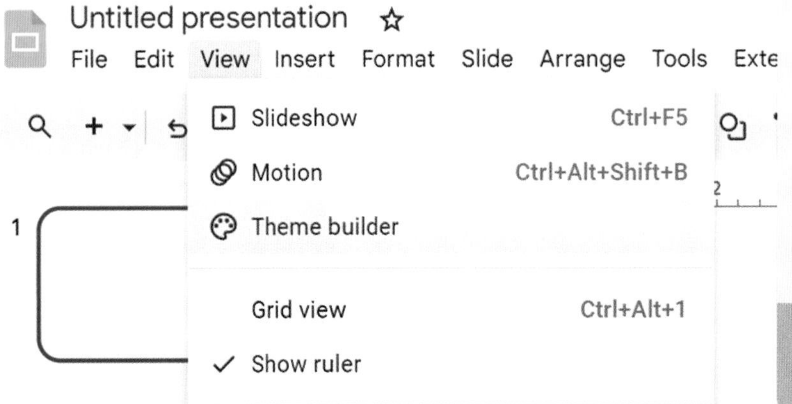

Figure 2.2.3 Opening a presentation theme builder.

You will then see the template. You can edit the template in the same way as you would edit any regular slide within a presentation. However, any changes you make to the colours and text styles will be automatically applied to all slides in the presentation once you exit the theme builder.

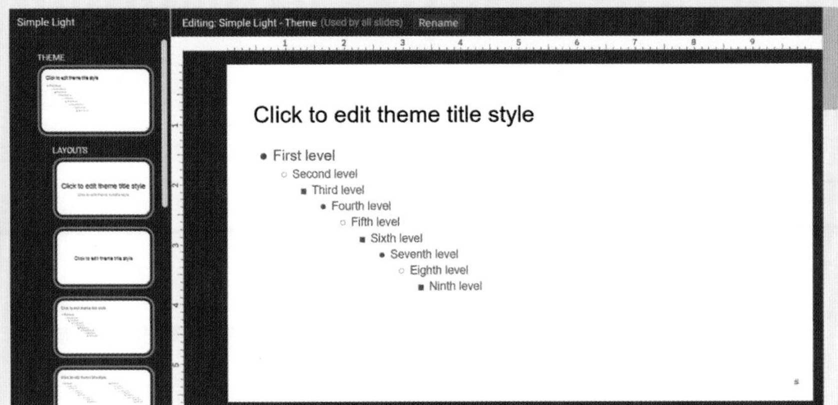

Figure 2.2.4 A typical presentation theme builder.

Workbook page 18: Complete Task A, '**What are the benefits of using a document template?**'.

> **Tip**
>
> Your presentation software probably comes with some pre-made template options you could select from, to quickly get started with creating a professional looking document.

Design a template for your virtual tour

Think about the features you would like the template for your virtual tour to have. You are going to create your tour using presentation software, so you need to come up with a design that will contain the features needed for every slide.

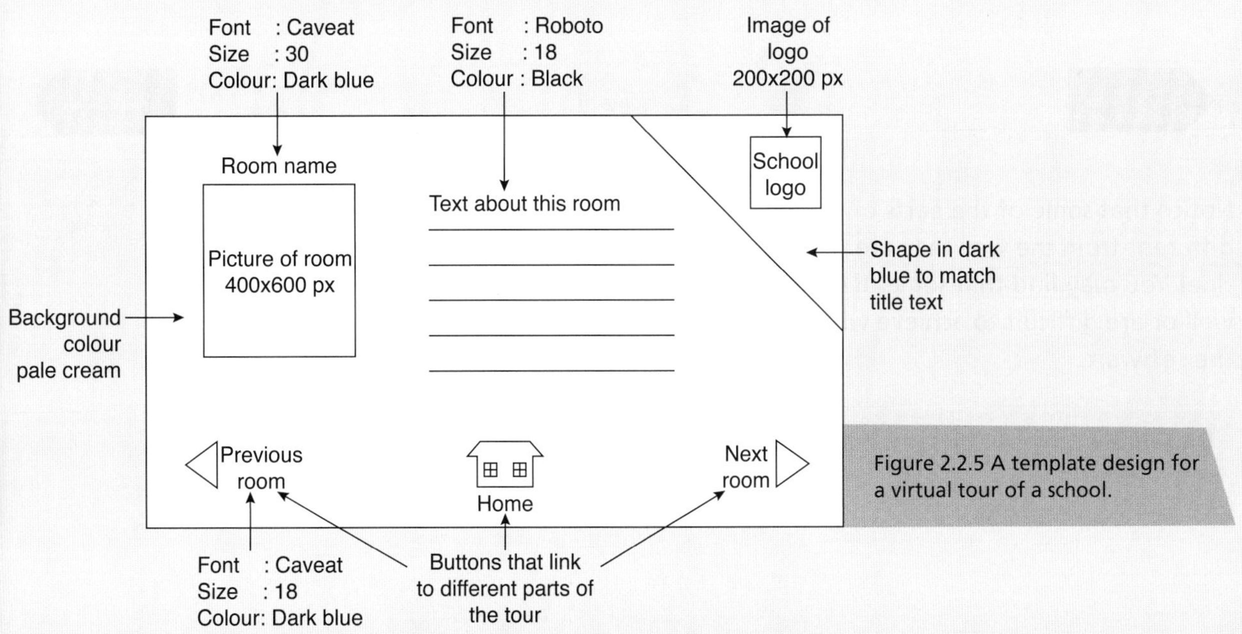

Figure 2.2.5 A template design for a virtual tour of a school.

Workbook page 19: Complete Task B, '**Draw your template design**'.

Build the template

Build 1:

With your partner, look at each other's template designs. You could choose one of the designs to recreate, or you may want to combine the best features from each template.

Using the skills you learned earlier in the lesson, create a single document template for your group's virtual tour using presentation software.

Here is an example of how the template may look once you have created it in the software:

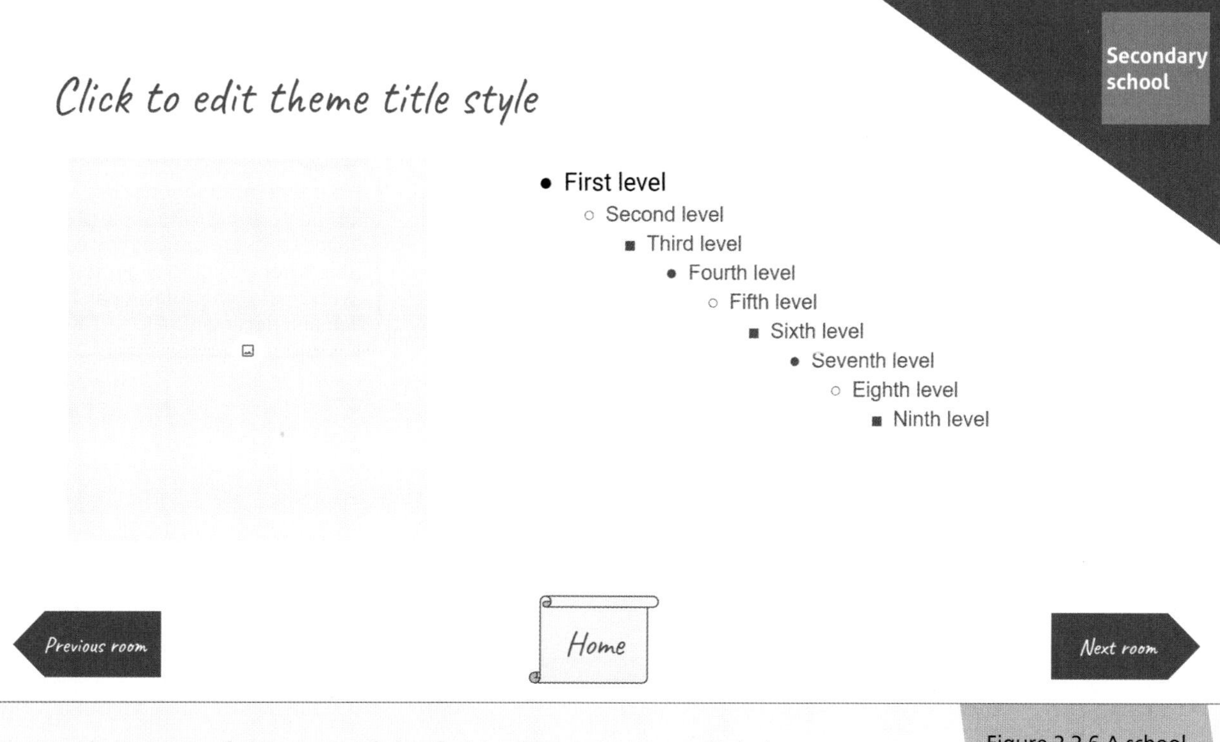

Figure 2.2.6 A school virtual tour theme.

Notice that some of the parts of the finished template are slightly different from the way they are featured in the design – this is fine! You may find that some of your design features don't work well or are difficult to achieve when you come to create them in the software.

Workbook page 19: Complete the '**Reflection**' task.

Chapter 2.3 Searching for information

What do we already know?

- How to search for information using a search engine

Key terms

Search term – the text you write into a search engine to find what you need

What information do I need?

You have a template for your virtual tour: now it needs some information. Look back at Workbook page 16: Task C: 'Plan your virtual tour' where you planned out the contents of your tour. With your partner, think about what extra information you will need, and where you might find this information.

Workbook page 21: Complete Task A, '**What extra information do you need?**'.

Researching information

You already know how to use a search engine to find information on the internet. Some things are more difficult to search for because the **search terms** used to describe them have multiple meanings.

If you type the search term 'rugby' into a search engine, you will probably get search results relating to the sport, which may be exactly what you wanted.

However, if you wanted to find out about the town in England called rugby (which was where the sport of rugby was invented), these results would not be very helpful.

You could type in 'rugby England' to narrow your search down, but this brings up results about the English national rugby team!

To find the extra information you need for your virtual tour, you can use some advanced search techniques to narrow down your search results.

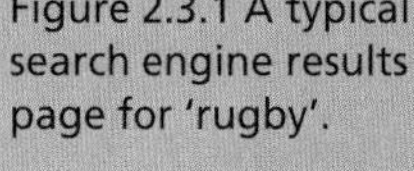

Figure 2.3.1 A typical search engine results page for 'rugby'.

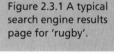

World Rugby
https://www.world.rugby › ...

World Rugby

The official site of World **Rugby** the governing body of **Rugby** Union with news, tournaments, fixtures, results, world **rugby** rankings, statistics, video, ...

Wikipedia

https://en.wikipedia.org › wiki › Rugby_union

Rugby union

Rugby is simply based on running with the ball in hand. In its most common form, a game is played between two teams of 15 players each, using an oval-shaped ...
History · Teams and positions · Laws and gameplay

England Rugby
https://www.englandrugby.com › ...

England Rugby

England beat Argentina in Bronze Medal Final · **Rugby** World Cup Fan Zone · YOUR LOCAL CLUB · Community **Rugby** Help Centre: find answers and ask questions on ...

Fixtures and Results
Fixtures and Results for the Rugby World Cup 2023.

Senior Men
The England Mens Senior Rugby Union team.

Fixtures & Results
40 players have been selected by England U18 Men's head coach ...

England
All England Teams Fixtures and Results · Senior Squads · More ...

More results from englandrugby.com »

Figure 2.3.2 Search engine results for 'rugby England'.

Improving search results

You can improve the quality of your search results by adding more information to your search terms.

Tip	Example search terms
Keywords – Social media posts often have hashtags to add relevant keywords. When you search, choose the relevant keywords for the information you want, just as you would in a social media post.	hair curly shampoo cat collar red kitten bell
Quotation marks – If you need to search for a specific phrase, put it in quotation marks so that the search engine searches for those words in that specific order.	"captain marvel" "how to" change tyre
Tilde – If you can't think of the right word, add a tilde (~) before a keyword, and some search engines will search for the word and its synonyms, a bit like a thesaurus.	television ~remote
Minus – If you want to specifically exclude a particular word from a search, use a minus sign in front of it.	cake -recipe band -hair

Some search engines have specific search modes to find images. If you click on the 'tools' button, there are additional filters to narrow down your search; for example, if you need a large image, or a particular file format.

Figure 2.3.3 Search engine categories.

All Images Videos Books Maps More Tools

Size Color Type Time Usage Rights

Stay safe

When you use a search engine, make sure that you type in appropriate search terms for the things you have been asked to research. Tell a teacher if you find anything that makes you feel uncomfortable.

Workbook page 21: Complete Task B, '**Web quest**'.

Build 2:

With your partner, split up the list you made in Workbook page 21: Task A, 'What extra information do you need?' and each gather some of the information. Collect the information in a rough document – do not add it to your virtual tour yet.

Some of the information you might need to find by searching the internet, and some might be things you already know and can type in.

Workbook page 22: Complete the '**Reflection**' task.

Chapter 2.4 Using multimedia

What do we already know?

- How to use sound, video, text and images to create a document

Key terms

Multimedia – using more than one method of presenting information, e.g. text, images, sound and/or video

What is multimedia?

Multimedia means using more than one method of presenting information. Your virtual tour may make use of a wide variety of media to make it more appealing.

Text

Figure 2.4.1 **Text** – written information about the location, labels to show different things on a photograph, or captions to describe a picture.

Images

Figure 2.4.2 **Images** – drawings or photographs to show different locations on the tour.

Sound

Figure 2.4.3 **Sound** – an interview with a relevant person, a voiceover, or a clip of a sound heard at the location.

Video

Figure 2.4.4 **Video** – to show what the location looks like, perhaps with a presenter talking about what can be seen.

It is important to choose the right media for the information you are presenting.

Workbook page 23: Complete Task A, '**What is it used for?**'.

Using technology safely

You have already collected some text and images to go with your virtual tour, but it is time to add some other media, such as video footage or sound recordings. What you can use will depend on what devices are available in your school.

Stay safe

When you are using multimedia devices such as cameras and microphones, you need to think about how to keep everyone, including you, safe.

Discuss 4

What rules do you think you and your classmates should agree to before you begin to collect content? As a class, agree on a set of guidelines for using multimedia, and note these down in your Workbook.

Workbook page 23: Complete Task B, '**Class guidelines for safe use of multimedia devices**'.

Gather some new material

Choose one or more of the types of multimedia described and gather some information in that format. The format you choose will depend on what devices are available for you to use. For example, you could use a sound recorder to interview another student, or you could take a digital photograph of an interesting part of your tour.

Figure 2.4.5 A digital photograph of a German village.

Figure 2.4.6 A video recording of dancers in Hyderabad, India.

Build 3:

Using the devices available to you, work with your partner to collect some new material to use in your virtual tour.

Workbook page 24: Complete the '**Reflection**' task.

Chapter 2.5 Presentation software

What do we already know?

- How to use standard features of presentation software

Key terms

Hotspot – an area on the screen that the user can click on to perform an action

Navigation – the way a user moves through a presentation or a website

Navigation

In this project, you are using presentation software to create a virtual tour. However, a virtual tour is not a presentation, as it will not be presented in person! Instead, the user needs to be able to control how they move through the tour, just as they would decide where to walk if they were actually visiting. The audience might be using these on a mobile device, a computer screen of a kiosk.

The example template design you saw earlier on in this project includes buttons to allow the user to navigate to different areas of the tour.

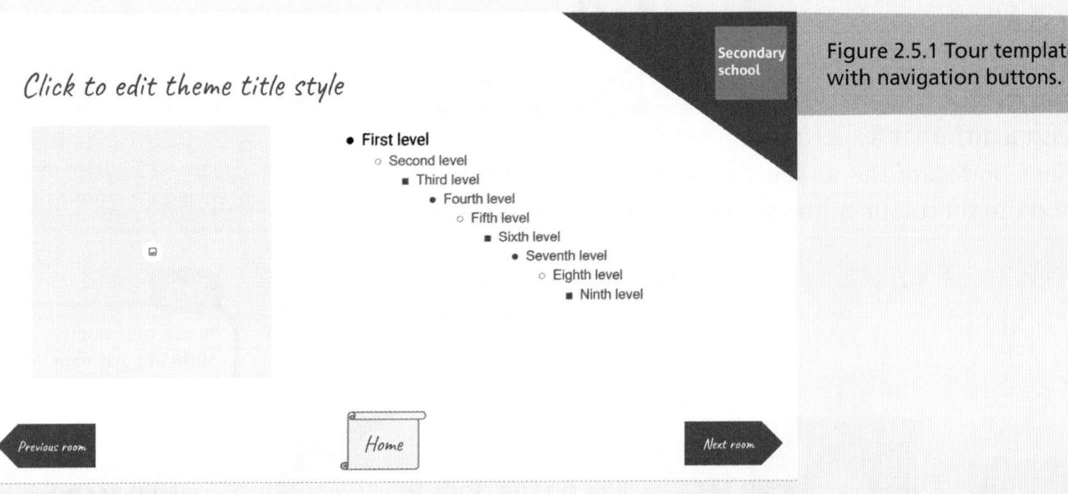

Figure 2.5.1 Tour template with navigation buttons.

Discuss 5

Can you foresee any problems with putting the buttons in the document template?

Think about how your user will **navigate** through your virtual tour. Will they move through in a specific order, or can they skip to a particular part of the tour? You could draw a diagram like the one on the right, to help you to work out which pages should link to each other.

Workbook page 25: Complete Task A, '**Navigation**'.

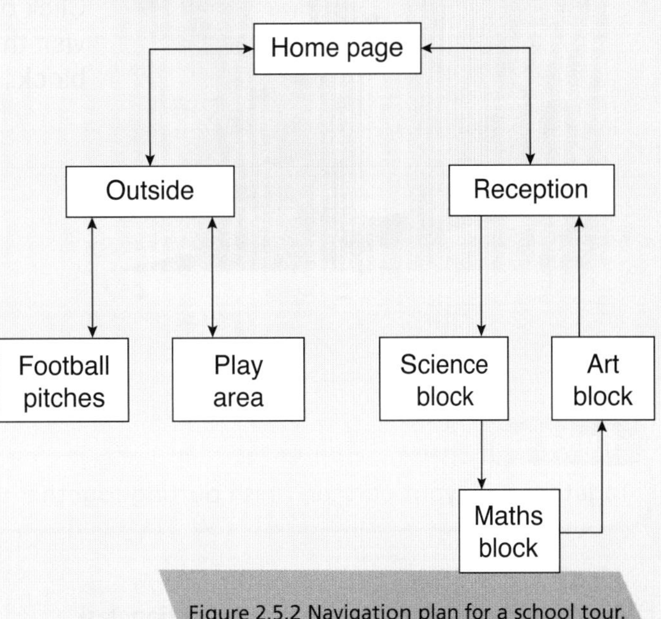

Figure 2.5.2 Navigation plan for a school tour.

Adding links

To allow the user to move between the different slides of your tour, the slides will need to contain links. The easiest way to add a link is to add a shape to your presentation, and then add a hyperlink to the shape. In the software shown here, you right click on the shape, select link and then select the slide you want it to link to.

A **hotspot** is an area on the screen that can be clicked on to perform an action. Clicking on a hotspot might link to another place, display a pop-up with some information, or even trigger a sound. A hotspot does not have to be visible. You could add a picture to your tour and then put an invisible hot spot on top of it. For example, you could have a picture of a door and then people on the tour would click the door to visit a different area. To do this, add a shape on top of the image, and make sure that both the outline and the fill colour of the shape are set to *transparent* or no fill.

Search

SLIDES

Next Slide

Previous Slide

First Slide

Last Slide

Slide 1: Home

Slide 2: Science block

Slide 3: Sports hall

Figure 2.5.2 Hyperlink navigation options.

Secondary school

Click on the door to visit the Science block...

Figure 2.5.3 Adding a hyperlink hotspot to an image.

Tip

If you give each slide in your tour a title, even if you have not filled in the information on that page yet, you will easily be able to see which slide to link to in the menu.

Build 4:

Together with your partner, finish putting together your tour using presentation software.

Workbook page 25: Complete the '**Reflection**' task.

Chapter 2.6 Augmented reality

What do we already know?

- Many smart devices have cameras which can be used by apps on the device

Key terms

Augmented reality – using technology to superimpose digital content on top of a real-world environment

Figure 2.6.1 An interview for a virtual tour.

Showcase your tour

Now that you have created your virtual tour, it is time to showcase your work to your class.

Showcase

Set up your virtual tour so that it is running, and other members of your class can try it out. Your teacher will tell you when it is your turn to test your classmates' tours. Imagine you are a judge awarding prizes to other students in your class for their work. Who would you award each of the prizes on the worksheet to?

What is augmented reality?

Augmented reality is the use of technology, including cameras, satellite positioning and object scanning, to superimpose digital content on top of a real-world environment.

Discuss 6

Can you think of any uses of augmented reality? Where might you have seen it used?

Augmented reality can be used for entertainment, for example in a scavenger hunt. Digital items are placed at real-world locations, and the player must travel to an actual location to be able to see and collect them using a smartphone camera and app to view the real world, with digital items overlaid on their screen.

Figure 2.6.1 Looking for dinosaurs with a smartphone augmented reality app.

Augmented reality has also become popular when designing rooms and choosing furniture. Some stores provide an augmented reality app to allow you to visualise what their furniture would look like in your own home before you buy it. This means that you can make decisions about expensive items with less risk that the item will not fit, or that you will not like how it looks once it is delivered.

Figure 2.6.2 Placing furniture in a room using augmented reality.

It is now possible to try on products that change your appearance, using augmented reality. For example, you can see what different shades of lipstick would look like, or what you would look like if you dyed your hair a different colour, before you buy the product. People can test products at home and purchase them online, and the risk of not being happy with the end result is reduced.

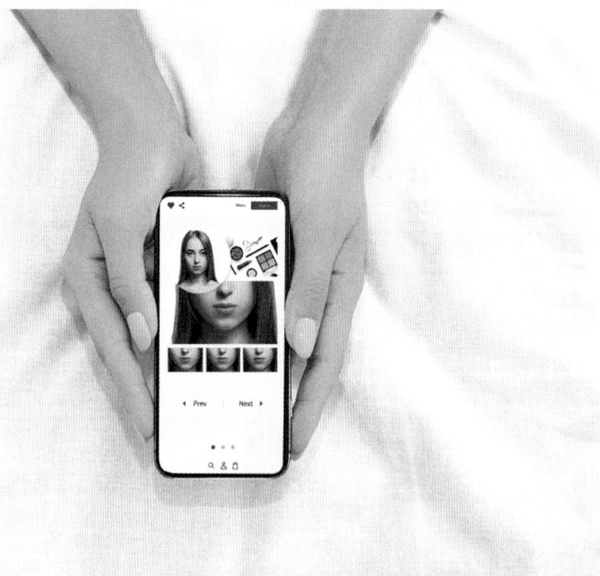

Figure 2.6.3 A mobile make-up simulation tool.

Workbook page 27: Complete task A, '**What are the benefits and drawbacks of augmented reality?**'.

Benefits and drawbacks of augmented reality

As with all technologies, augmented reality has both benefits and drawbacks. The technology is relatively new, so it is evolving and improving at a rapid pace.

In healthcare, augmented reality can be used to visualise how a drug works in the body, to help a surgeon perform an operation, and to train new doctors and nurses.

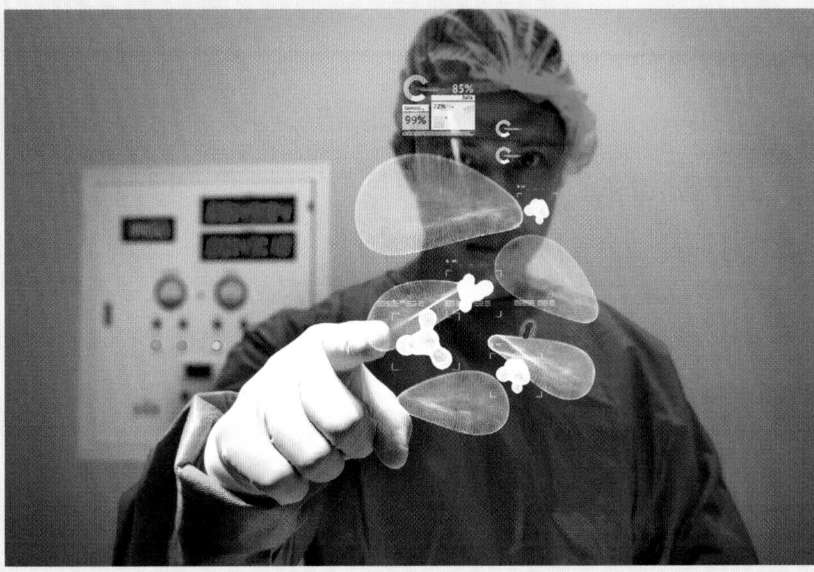

Figure 2.6.4 Using augmented reality to support a medical operation.

Medical students benefit from using augmented reality apps to improve their practical skills and increase their knowledge, without causing risk to a patient. Simulating a real operation environment also helps people to learn skills such as working collaboratively and reacting to a simulated crisis situation. However, regardless of how good the augmented reality simulation is, it is never the same as working with a real human patient.

Using augmented reality to help you to shop for new clothes can be helpful, because it means you do not need to travel to an actual shop to try things on and can order what you need online. However, although it can show you what new clothes or shoes would look like to wear, it is not possible to test how they fit using augmented reality and this may result in frustration if your new items don't fit, and an ecological impact if items are continually ordered and then returned.

Workbook page 28: Complete the '**Reflection**' task.

Figure 2.6.5 Trying on shoes using an augmented reality app.

Congratulations!

Well done! You have completed Chapter 2, 'Content creation'.

In this chapter you:

- ☑ thought about the audience for a piece of work
- ☑ created a template for a document
- ☑ learned how to search more effectively
- ☑ created some multimedia content
- ☑ used presentation software to create an interactive tour
- ☑ showcased your work to the class
- ☑ explored augmented reality.

Key terms

Audience – the people who will look at the work you produce

Augmented reality – using technology to superimpose digital content on top of a real-world environment

Emoji – a small icon used in text to express an emotion or represent an item

GIF – an image format that allows animation

Hotspot – an area on the screen that the user can click on to perform an action

Meme – a familiar image, often accompanied with text, which is shared and reused on the internet

Multimedia – using more than one method of presenting information, e.g. text, images, sound and/or video

Navigation – the way a user moves through a presentation or a website

Search term – the text you write into a search engine to find what you need

Template – a pre-designed format for a document

Virtual tour – a simulation of being at a particular location, involving multimedia such as images, text and perhaps also sound and video

Reflect: What can you do now that you couldn't do before?

Chapter 3 Create with code 1

Project: Fantasy name generator

In this chapter, you will:

- write Python code directly into an editor as text
- predict what an algorithm will do and test whether you were right
- use variables and constants
- use a program library to generate random numbers and choose random items from a list
- break a program into smaller parts to make it easier to code
- improve your program in stages by gradually adding more features.

End of chapter project: Fantasy name generator

You may have read books or watched films where the characters have fantastical names such as "Fearless Nazir, musician of Lavaland". You are going to create a program which will generate a randomly chosen fantasy name and tell a short story about your new character.

Figure 3.0.1 A fantasy character.

Chapter 3.1 Familiarisation with Python

What do we already know?

- How to use inputs, outputs and variables in a blocks-based programming language (e.g. Scratch or EduBlocks)

Key terms

Concatenation – joining two or more pieces of text together

Text-based programming language – allows you to type text instructions that a computer can run

String – a sequence of characters, numbers and/or punctuation, usually written within quotation marks

In fantasy films and TV shows, characters often have exciting names and titles like "Fearless Stompenchomp, the Dragonslayer" or "Princess Twinklewings of Fairylandia". In this lesson you will write a program to generate some fictional names – perhaps you could use them in your next story?

Using Python

In this lesson you are going to use a text-based programming language called Python. You have previously used EduBlocks, where you could drag blocks into place to write a Python program. However, Python is a **text-based programming language,** and during this chapter you will learn how to type the program commands yourself and save them into a file.

Build 1:

Open the Python programming environment you are using (ask your teacher if you are not sure how to do this).

Here is a very short and simple Python program.

```
print("Hello world")
```

Type in the program, save it and then run it. You should see the text "Hello world" displayed on your screen.

Fill in the table in your Workbook so that you remember the correct instructions to write, save and run a program. If you forget, you can come back to this page for a reminder.

Workbook page 30: Complete Task A, '**Writing a Python program**'.

Tip

If you don't see the message 'Hello world', first check that you have typed in the program correctly without missing any brackets or quotation marks. Check that you have typed your program in the correct place. If you see an error message, read it and see if you can work out what it means before asking for help.

Discuss 1

Did the program do what you expected it to? What do you think the command `print` means in Python?

The `print` command in Python is similar to the `say` command in Scratch.

Scratch	Python
say Hello! Figure 3.1.1 The Scratch 'say' block.	`print("Hello!")`

Inputs and outputs

All programs have some form of input and some form of output, and you have written programs with both inputs and outputs before in block-based languages. Now compare what inputs look like in Python compared with Scratch.

Scratch	Python
ask What is your name? and wait Figure 3.1.2 A Scratch input block.	`answer = input("What is your name? ")`

In Scratch, you would see the output in a speech bubble, and a box to type in, like this:

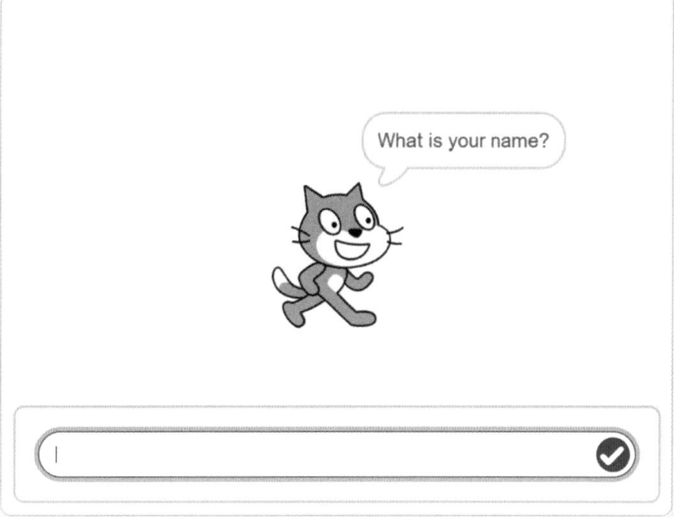

Figure 3.1.3 A Scratch sprite output bubble.

Build 2:

Type in and run the Python code from the table above. What happens?

Workbook page 30: Complete Task B, '**Recreate the Scratch program**'.

Variables

answer = input (" What is your name? ")

Variable name — Command to allow the user to type something — Instructions so that the user knows what to type

Figure 3.1.4 A breakdown of a Python input function.

Now take a closer look at the piece of code you have already used for getting some input in Python in Figure 3.1.4.

Did you notice that this line of code contains a variable called `answer` as well as an input command? Remember that a variable is somewhere you can store a piece of data to refer to it later in the program. In this case, the piece of data is the person's name.

But what if you want to save more than one piece of data at once? You can create more than one variable, but each must have its own name.

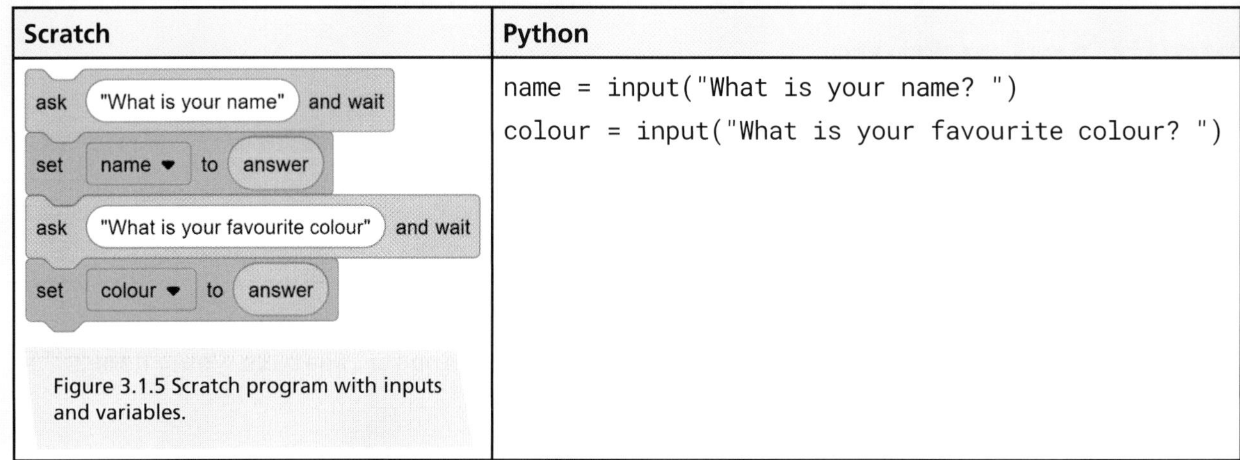
ask "What is your name" and wait
set name to answer
ask "What is your favourite colour" and wait
set colour to answer

Scratch	Python
Figure 3.1.5 Scratch program with inputs and variables.	`name = input("What is your name? ")` `colour = input("What is your favourite colour? ")`

You can then refer to the variable later in the program.

```
name = input("What is your name? ")
print("Hello " + name )
```

In most programming languages, a piece of text is called a **string**. Joining strings together is called **concatenation**, and in Python you do this with a + symbol. You can join as many strings together as you like; it doesn't matter whether they are strings you have written yourself or strings that have been stored as variables.

```
print( "Hello " + name + " lovely to meet you")
```

Build 3:

Adapt your program so that it creates at least two variables, collects data from the user to populate them, and then writes a response using each piece of data. For example your program might say `"Wow, Rayan is a cool name"` or `"I like blue too!"`

Tip

Make sure you give each variable a sensible and unique name that describes the data it contains.

Tip

You can choose any name for a variable, as long as the name begins with a letter and it does not contain any spaces. Instead of spaces, you can use underscores, e.g. `player_name`

Tip

If you are concatenating data from a variable into a sentence, remember that you will need to add the spaces yourself. The code `print("Hello" + name)` will result in the output `HelloRayan` if you type in the name Rayan!

To fix this, add a space after Hello, but within the quotation marks, like this: `print("Hello " + name)`

Funny story game

Role play 1

In groups of four, play the funny story game.

You have already learned enough Python to create your own funny story game. You can use input commands to ask the user some questions, store their answers in variables and then concatenate the data from the variables together with text that you have written to create a story.

Build 4:

Using a maximum of four inputs, design and build your own funny story game in Python.

Stay safe

Remember to be kind in your story – it is supposed to be funny, not insulting or embarrassing. Make sure you write a story that you would be happy to star in yourself.

Workbook page 31: Complete the '**Reflection**' task.

Discuss 2

Share some of the similarities and differences you spotted between Scratch and Python.

Chapter 3.2 Program library

What do we already know?

- How to concatenate (join) two strings together
- The features of a strong password, such as length, range of characters and randomness

Key terms

List – a data structure which can hold more than one piece of data

Program library – a collection of pre-written code which can be imported and used within another program

Random – chosen by chance

What is a program library?

Programmers don't usually write code for things that someone else has already worked out how to do. Instead, they use code from a program library to get them started, and then write their own code to customise the parts that matter to them. A **program library** is a collection of pre-written code that can be imported and used within another program.

Video game programmers may use library code for common tasks, such as making a character move left and right, climbing ladders or moving items such as boxes. They would write their own code for custom tasks such as making the character do a special move.

Workbook page 32: Complete task A, '**Video game program library**'.

What common tasks might the programmer of this platform-based video game use a program library for?

Figure 3.2.1 A simple platform video game.

Discuss 3

Share your ideas with the class.

Why use a program library?

Program libraries are useful because they:

- save time – you don't have to write all of your code from scratch
- allow you to perform complicated tasks
- run quickly and efficiently; for example, a search function from a library is likely to be much more efficient than one you write yourself.

The random library

Python, along with most programming languages, comes with lots of pre-written library code that you can use in your programs. In this unit, you are going to use a program library called `random`.

The word **random** means chosen by chance. All of the functions in the random library involve asking the computer to randomly select something.

The command to import the random library looks like this, and you should write it exactly *once*, at the start of your program.

```
import random
```

The random library has a variety of functions you can use. Once you have added the code to import the library at the start of your program, you can use any of the functions in your code, like this:

```
print( random.randint(1, 6) )
```

The `random.randint` part of the code tells Python to look in the 'random' program library and use the 'randint' (short for 'random integer') function that it finds there.

Workbook page 32: Complete task B, '**Guess what this code does**'.

Choose a random item from a list

The random library has another function that can choose a random item from a list for you.

Tip

If you try to concatenate (join) your random number to a string, you will run into an error.

```
number = random.randint(1, 6) print( "The number was " + number )
```

This code gives the error *"TypeError: can only concatenate str (not "int") to str"*. This is because you can only concatenate a string to another string. To fix it, convert (cast) your randomly generated number to a string like this:

```
number = random.randint(1, 6) print( "The number was " + str(number) )
```

Build 5:

Start a new program file, then type in and run the code to find out what the computer thinks you should have to drink.

```
import random
drinks = ["water", "juice", "cola", "lemonade"]
print(random.choice(drinks))
```

This program uses a **list**, which is a data structure that can hold more than one piece of data. In this program you can see a list of strings. Items in the list are written within the square brackets [ ], and the whole list is given the name `drinks`. The program uses the `choice` function from the `random` library to choose one of the drinks at random from the list.

Random password generator

When you need to use a username and password to access an online account, you will usually have to provide a username and a password. Sometimes it can be difficult to think of a password that meets the criteria for the website! You will often be asked to include at least one number, one letter and one special character in the password you choose.

Figure 3.2.2 Finding a strong password.

Password	Password	Password
•••••	•••••••	••••••••••
weak	medium	strong

Build 6:

Design and build a password generator program to generate a strong password. Your password should include letters, a number and a special character (e.g. *, &, £, @ etc.)

You will need to combine lots of the skills you have learned so far to complete this program. Here is your brief:

- Generate a random number, and save it in a variable
- Ask the user to type in a letter, and save it in a variable
- Generate a random special character from a list, and save it in a variable

You can combine and print the values you have saved by listing them with commas in a print statement like this. Number, letter, and special are the names of the variables, so if you have used different variable names you will need to update your code.

```
print(number, letter, special)
```

Tip

If you want to include more characters in your password, create additional variables with numbers, for example number1, number2.

Stay safe

Never tell anyone your real password, even your friends!

Workbook page 33: Complete the '**Reflection**' task.

Chapter 3.3 Decomposition

What do we already know?

- How to draw a flowchart to design an algorithm

Key terms

Decomposition – the process of breaking down a complex problem into smaller, more manageable tasks

Learning how to play a new sport can be difficult. If you wanted to learn how to play football, you probably wouldn't start by playing in a match! Instead, the coach might show you how to do individual skills, such as running with the ball, passing it to another player and shooting.

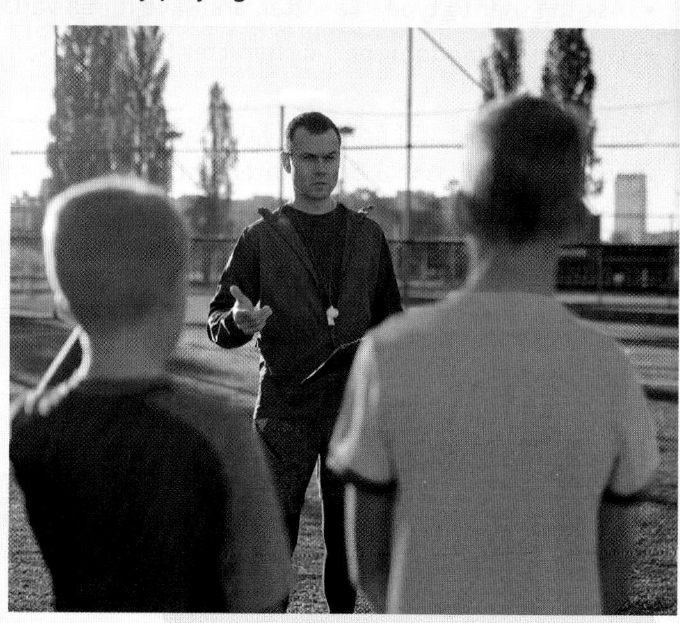

Figure 3.3.1 Students learning to play football.

What is decomposition?

Decomposition means to break down a complex task into smaller, more manageable tasks. It is a technique used by programmers when they are writing complex programs.

Think of a game you like to play and imagine you want to teach a friend how to play the game. What are the different parts of the game? Do any of the parts have sub-parts?

Figure 3.3.2 Friends playing congkak.

Figure 3.2.3 Children playing popular skipping games in Qatar.

Workbook page 34: Complete Task A, '**Decompose a game**'.

Decompose a problem

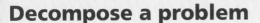

Project brief

You are going to design a program to randomly generate a fantasy name for yourself. You will:

- think about the different parts of the name
- decompose the task into several smaller tasks
- plan each part using a flowchart before writing the code
- test and debug your program to check that it works
- add extra features based on feedback you receive on your program

In fantasy books and films, characters often have a name with several parts, like this:

- Fearless Nazir, musician of Lavaland
- Cheerful Asma, builder of Azimuth

This might seem like a difficult task, especially as you have only just started programming with Python. To make a difficult programming task easier, you can decompose it into smaller parts.

Workbook page 34: Complete Task B, '**What's in a name?**'.

Design each part

Now that you have broken down the fantasy name into four parts, you can plan how your name generator program will work. For each part separately, think about:

- Will this part of the name be randomly chosen from a list, or will the user type it in?
- If it is randomly chosen, what will be the list of possible values to choose from?

You can then draw a flowchart to design how that part of the program will work. Here is an example flowchart for the first part of the name:

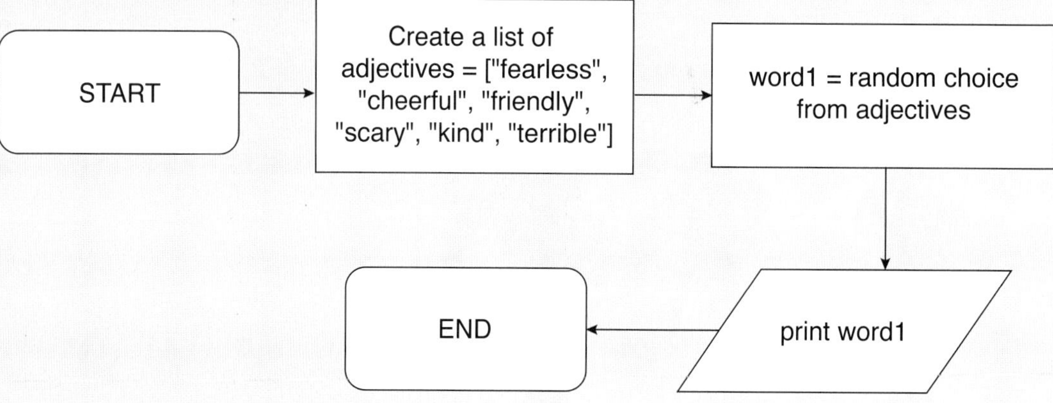

Figure 3.3.4 A flowchart containing a list.

Design 1

On paper, plan the remaining three parts of the program, each as a separate flowchart.

Put it back together

It is important to also consider how the different parts you have designed will fit together to create the finished program, and whether you will need to add any extra parts to join them together.

Design 2

Plan the whole program as one single flowchart.

Workbook page 35: Complete the '**Reflection**' task.

Chapter 3.4 Name generator

What do we already know?

- How to use the random library to choose a random string from a list

Key terms

Constant – a value that does not change while the program is running

Comment – a note written for a human to read in a program. All comments are completely ignored by the computer

What changes?

Here is some code for choosing a random season from a list.

```
import random
seasons = ["spring", "summer", "autumn", "winter"]
result = random.choice(seasons)
```

Figure 3.4.1 Four seasons.

Discuss 4

Name the two variables in this piece of code. Which variable contains data that stays the same every time the program is run, and which variable contains a different value each time?

Using constants

A value that does not change while the program is running is called a **constant**. The names of constants are usually written in uppercase letters, to show that they are different from variables, which are written in lowercase. Here are some examples of constants:

```
PI = 3.14159
MONTHS = ["Jan", "Feb", "Mar", "Apr", "May", "Jun",
"Jul", "Aug", "Sep", "Oct", "Nov", "Dec"]
```

Discuss 5

Compare these two programs for calculating the area of a pizza and the amount of money saved by using a discount. They have the same result, but one of them uses constants and one does not.

Which program is clearer, and why?

Program 1	Program 2
diameter = input("Diameter in cm: ") price = int(input("Price: ")) radius = int(diameter) / 2 area = radius * radius * 3.14159 moneyoff = price * 0.1 print("Pizza area " + str(area)) print("Discount " + str(moneyoff))	DISCOUNT = 0.1 PI = 3.14159 diameter = input("Diameter in cm: ") price = int(input("Price: ")) radius = int(diameter) / 2 area = radius * radius * PI moneyoff = price * DISCOUNT print("Pizza area " + str(area)) print("Discount " + str(moneyoff))

Workbook page 36: Complete Task A, '**Constants**'.

Design 3

Go back to your flowchart design from last lesson and annotate on the design whether each piece of data should be stored as a variable or a constant.

Use comments

Almost all programmers use **comments** in their programs. A comment is a note written for a human to read in a program. All comments are completely ignored by the computer when the program is run – their only purpose is to help humans to understand the code.

To write a comment in Python, add a # symbol and then write your comment.

```
# Ask the user to type in the price of the pizza
price = int(input("Price: "))
```

Figure 3.4.2 A student using Python.

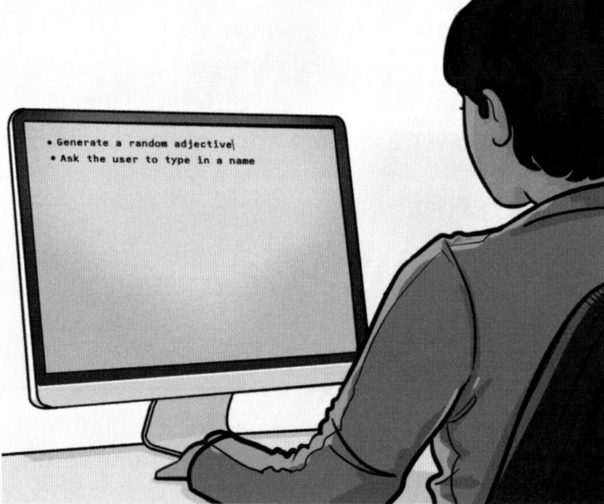

Build 7:

Start a new Python program. Go through the flowchart you drew in the previous lesson and add one comment to the program for each box in the flowchart.

Write the name generator program

Build 8:

Go back to the start of the program and write program code underneath each comment to complete that task. Test your code as you go and fix any errors.

Tip

Comments can be used as a tool, either to note down a task that needs to be done *before* the code is written or to explain code *after* it has been written.

Workbook page 36: Complete the '**Reflection**' task.

Chapter 3.5 Story generator

What do we already know?

- How to debug a program, for example by running it after adding a new feature and checking that it still works

A random story

In this lesson, you are going to use the skills you have already learned to put together a randomly generated story about your character. You already know some information about your character – they have a randomly chosen adjective to describe their personality, they have a randomly chosen job and they come from a randomly chosen made-up place.

You could use these pieces of information to start off your new story, for example:

```
print(name + " was fed up with being a " + job)
```

This code writes a different sentence each time, for example your output might be:

`Nazir was fed up with being a musician` or `Asma was fed up with being a builder`

To make your story more interesting, you need to add more randomly generated information. For example, your story might involve your character going on a quest to find an item:

```
QUEST_ITEMS = ["special crystal", "golden stone", "power stone"]
item = random.choice(QUEST_ITEMS)
```

So the first line of your story might look something like this:

```
print(name + " decided to leave " + place + " and
go on a quest to find a " + item)
```

This code might give the following output:

```
Nazir decided to leave Lavaland and go on a quest
to find a special crystal
```

Note down in your Workbook some ideas for new parts of a story. You don't have to write about a quest, you can choose your own idea for a story.

Workbook page 38: Complete Task A, '**Design your story**'.

Figure 3.5.1 Quest items

Debugging

Python is a fairly new programming language, and the error messages it produces may seem difficult to understand. However, with a bit of practice, you can learn how to read them and understand what they mean, so you can fix problems with your program.

You have already practised debugging programs in block-based programming languages, and you know that it is a good idea to stop when you add each new feature to your program, and run the program to check whether it still works.

Here is an example of a Python error message, with some annotation to show the different parts of the message.

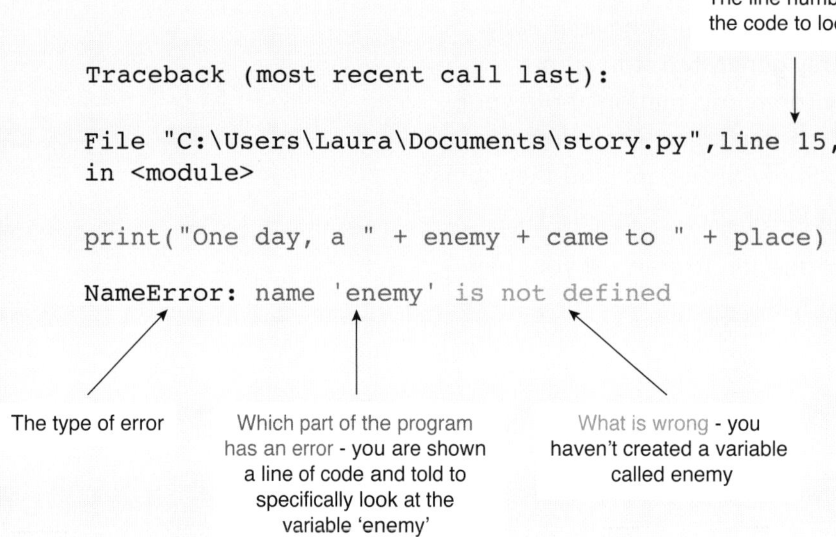
The line number of the code to look at
Traceback (most recent call last):
File "C:\Users\Laura\Documents\story.py",line 15, in <module>
print("One day, a " + enemy + came to " + place)
NameError: name 'enemy' is not defined
The type of error
Which part of the program has an error - you are shown a line of code and told to specifically look at the variable 'enemy'
What is wrong - you haven't created a variable called enemy

Python gives you a lot of information in the error message, but you still need to do some detective work to figure out what has caused the error. In this example, Python cannot find a variable called 'enemy', which you have referred to on line 15 of your program. This might be because you have forgotten to create the variable, or it might be because you have spelled the variable name wrongly, or it could be for another different reason.

Workbook page 38: Complete Task B, '**What does the error message mean?**'.

Tell your story

Build 9:

Save a separate copy of your name generator program, so that you have working code you can go back to if necessary.

Add new code to the second copy of your program to tell a story about your character. Remember to save and run this new program each time you add a new feature, to check that it still works.

Tip

You can add comments just like you did during the previous lesson to help you to plan the new parts of your code

Workbook page 39: Complete the '**Reflection**' task.

Chapter 3.6 Feedback on software

Real software developers regularly check the code that other developers have written – this is called a **code review**. Developers also ask for feedback from users of the software they are developing and use it to improve the software. In this lesson, you will take on both of these roles to give some feedback to your classmates.

Key terms

Code review – a software developer checking code written by another developer and suggesting improvements

Iterative development – regularly adding new features and improvements to a piece of software, and then seeking feedback to inform the next set of improvements

User feedback – feedback from a person who uses a piece of software

Code review

Large pieces of software are not usually written all at once. Instead, different parts are worked on by different developers, and then combined to create the finished product. Updates and new features are also developed separately, and only added to the finished working piece of software once they have been checked by another developer.

Code reviews help developers to improve the quality of the code they write. You are going to code review your partner's code, but first you need to decide what features of the code to focus on.

Here are some of the things you have learned about during this unit:

- Using constants
- Sensible variable names
- Comments
- Are there any bugs in the code – does the code run properly?

Figure 3.6.1 Software developers working together.

Discuss 6

As a class, discuss and decide which features you want code reviewers to comment on in your code review.

Workbook page 40: Complete Task A , '**Code review focus**'.

Showcase

Open your code and then swap computers and Workbooks with your partner. Review their code and write suggestions for how they could improve the code in the table.

Workbook page 40: Task B, '**Review the code**'.

User feedback

Figure 3.6.2 Programmer having received positive user feedback.

User feedback is feedback given to a developer by a person who uses a piece of software. You are going to play the role of a 'user' and give feedback on your classmate's program.

Normally a software user will have little or no understanding of how the software was built, so they do not comment on the code itself, only the running program.

A user of your story program might comment on:

- anything that isn't working properly or doesn't make sense
- spelling mistakes or missing spaces between words
- the quality of the story
- the variety of different stories you can generate

Discuss 7

As a class, discuss and decide which features of the program you will give user feedback on.

Workbook page 41: Complete Task C , '**User feedback focus**'.

Showcase

Open your code and then swap computers and Workbooks with your partner. Run the code and write suggestions in the table for how they could improve the program.

Workbook page 41: Task D, '**Give user feedback**'.

Iterative development

Software developers often follow a process called **iterative development**. They regularly add small new features and improvements from their software, reviewing each other's code before it is released. Once each new improvement is released, they ask users for feedback which they use to inform their next set of improvements.

Build 10:

Return to your own computer and review the feedback you have been given. Make changes to your code, if necessary, to implement some of the recommendations from the feedback – you do not need to act on all the feedback, and you may not even agree with some of it!

Workbook page 42: Complete the '**Reflection**' task.

Well done! **You have completed Chapter 3, 'Create with code 1'.**

In this chapter you:

- ☑ used a new programming language called Python
- ☑ used the 'random' program library to generate random numbers and choose random items from a list
- ☑ planned your program by decomposing it into smaller parts
- ☑ used constants for values that do not change while the program is running
- ☑ wrote a program to generate a fantasy character name, and a fantasy story
- ☑ code reviewed a classmate's code and provided user feedback.

Key terms

Code review – a software developer checking code written by another developer and suggesting improvements

Comment – a note written for a human to read in a program. All comments are completely ignored by the computer

Concatenation – joining two or more pieces of text together

Constant – a value that does not change while the program is running

Decomposition – the process of breaking down a complex problem into smaller, more manageable tasks

Iterative development – regularly adding new features and improvements to a piece of software, and then seeking feedback to inform the next set of improvements

List – a data structure that can hold more than one piece of data

Program library – a collection of pre-written code that can be imported and used within another program

Random – chosen by chance

String – a sequence of letters, numbers and/or punctuation, usually written within quotation marks

Text-based language – allows you to type text instructions that a computer can run

User feedback – feedback from a person who uses a piece of software

Reflect: What can you do now that you couldn't do before? Do you prefer writing code in a text-based language or a blocks-based language?

Chapter 4 How computers work

Project: Troubleshooter

In this chapter, you will:

- learn about your computer's main memory – RAM and ROM
- find out what the operating system of your computer controls
- investigate how antivirus and other utilities help keep your computer working
- learn how a firewall protects your network
- understand why different people can access different files
- think about the risks and benefits of connecting devices to a network
- create a troubleshooter to find and resolve a wide range of computer problems.

End of chapter project: Troubleshooter

Just like a doctor learns about human biology so that they can diagnose diseases, if you know how your computer works, you can use this information to sort out any problems. In this chapter, you will learn about various parts of the computer, and then combine this knowledge to create a troubleshooter guide that provides advice to help with a computer problem.

Figure 4.0.1 Technician using a troubleshooting flowchart.

Chapter 4.1 Memory

What do we already know?

- How to follow a flowchart
- Secondary storage (e.g. a hard drive), is used to store files and documents

Key terms

Troubleshooter – a tool or guide that gathers information to pinpoint the cause of a problem, and then offers advice on how to fix it

RAM – Random Access Memory, used to store instructions and data the computer is currently working with. Contents are lost when the power is switched off

ROM – Read Only Memory, stores the instructions needed to load the operating system. Contents are kept when the power is switched off

A **troubleshooter** is a tool that gathers information to pinpoint the cause of a problem, and then offers advice on how to fix it. It works a little bit like a flowchart, because it asks a series of questions to rule out possible causes of the problem.

Workbook page 44: Complete Task A, '**Classify the animals**'.

Types of troubleshooter

When you are ill, you or whoever is looking after you can type your symptoms into a type of troubleshooter called a symptom checker, to find out what kind of illness you might have. The symptom checker will then offer you advice about what to do, including whether you need to book an appointment to see a doctor.

Computer troubleshooting tools ask a series of questions and may ask you to change settings on the computer, for example, to turn a switch on or off. The tool then shows you what it thinks is the problem and offers advice on how to fix it.

Symptoms

Symptom Checker

About this Symptom Checker

When to seek medical advice

Get emergency medical care if your child's headache:

- Is sudden and severe or the "worst headache ever"
- Is accompanied by a fever, nausea or vomiting not related to a known illness
- Is accompanied by a stiff neck, rash, confusion, seizures, double vision, weakness, numbness or difficulty speaking
- Follows a head injury, fall or bump

Get prompt medical care if your child's headache:

- Gets worse despite rest and over-the-counter pain medication

1 Choose a symptom | 2 Select related factors | 3 View possible causes

Headaches in children

Find possible causes of headaches based on specific factors. Check one or more factors on this page that apply to your child's symptom.

Pain is

- ☐ Intense
- ☐ Mild to moderate
- ☐ Moderate to severe
- ☐ Pressure or squeezing sensation
- ☐ Stabbing or burning
- ☐ Throbbing

Pain located

- ☐ Around one eye or radiates from one eye
- ☐ On both sides of head
- ☐ On one side of head

Onset is

- ☐ Gradual
- ☐ Preceded by a head injury or fall
- ☐ Preceded by frequent use of pain medication
- ☐ Preceded by visual or other sensory disturbances
- ☐ Sudden

Figure 4.1.1 A medical troubleshooting tool.

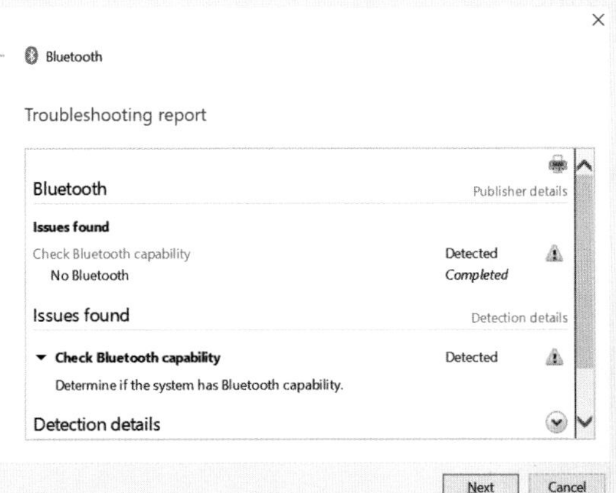

Figure 4.1.2 A troubleshooting report

Discuss 1

Where have you seen a troubleshooter before?

In this unit, you will create your own tool to troubleshoot computer problems. Before you start, you will learn a bit more about how your computer works so that your tool can offer helpful advice.

ROM and RAM

You already know that when you turn your computer off at the end of the day, and come back to it the next day, your files are still there waiting for you. This is because your files are stored on a secondary storage device such as a hard disk drive or a solid state drive.

Your computer has two other types of memory – **ROM** and **RAM**.

ROM stands for Read Only Memory, which means that it contains some instructions and data that can be looked at (read) but cannot be changed. ROM is used to store the very important instructions needed to load the software needed to start your computer. Without ROM, your computer would not be able to start when turned on.

Figure 4.1.3 A ROM microchip.

RAM stands for Random Access Memory, which means that any part of the memory can be accessed at any time. RAM stores the instructions and data that the computer is currently working on. The computer can access the data in its RAM very quickly compared with data stored in secondary storage. However, when the computer's power is switched off, the contents of RAM are erased.

Figure 4.1.4 A RAM microchip.

How does the computer use RAM?

All computers contain a processor that fetches and runs the instructions needed to make the software work. The processor uses the RAM as a 'working memory' area, to store data it is currently using so that it can find it again quickly. However, RAM is relatively expensive, so its storage capacity is much smaller than your hard drive.

Role play 1

To demonstrate how RAM works, you are going to take part in a role-play exercise in pairs. You will need five different coloured pencils or pens. You will also need the pictures in the Workbook page 45:Task B, 'Memory role play'.

- One person holds all of the pencils – this person is the *secondary storage*.
- The other person will do the colouring – they represent the *processor*. This person can keep up to two pencils on their desk – the desk represents the *RAM*.

How does RAM affect your computer's performance?

Discuss 2

In the role play exercise:

- Which was faster – retrieving from RAM or from secondary storage?
- Which instructions in the sequence were processed fastest?
- What effect did increasing the amount of RAM have on how quickly the task was finished?

Write some questions

Build 1:

Now that you know about the different types of memory, you can start to write some questions for your own troubleshooter. You will need to use flowchart software – your teacher will tell you which one to use. Here is an example of a flowchart that has been started, with some questions about memory. You can use these questions as a starting point, or make up your own.

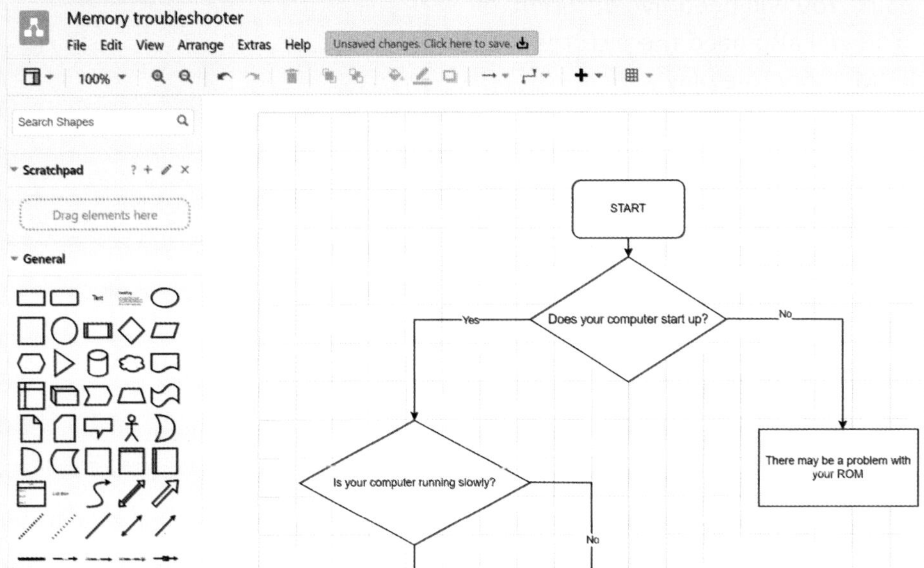

Figure 4.1.5 An example of flowchart software.

Make sure that you use the correct flowchart symbols. Here is a reminder:

START	Does the computer turn on?	Information	——— YES ———→
Start or end	Decision	Information about the problem or a suggestion for how to solve it	Labelled arrows for yes or no decisions

Workbook page 46: Complete the '**Reflection**' task.

Chapter 4.2 The operating system

What do we already know?

- ROM contains the instructions needed to load the operating system
- The contents of ROM are kept when the power is switched off

Key terms

Application software – allows the computer user to do a task, for example a web browser or a word processor

Driver – a small piece of software that allows the operating system to communicate with a hardware device such as a printer

Operating system (OS) – an important piece of software that manages all other software and hardware devices

Utility software – keeps the computer secure and in working order, for example antivirus software

What is an operating system?

Every computer needs an **operating system** to be able to function. The operating system (often just called the OS for short) is an important piece of software that manages all the computer's other software as well as its hardware devices. You have probably heard of some common operating systems such as Windows, Linux and Mac OS on personal computers, and iOS and Android on mobile phones and tablets.

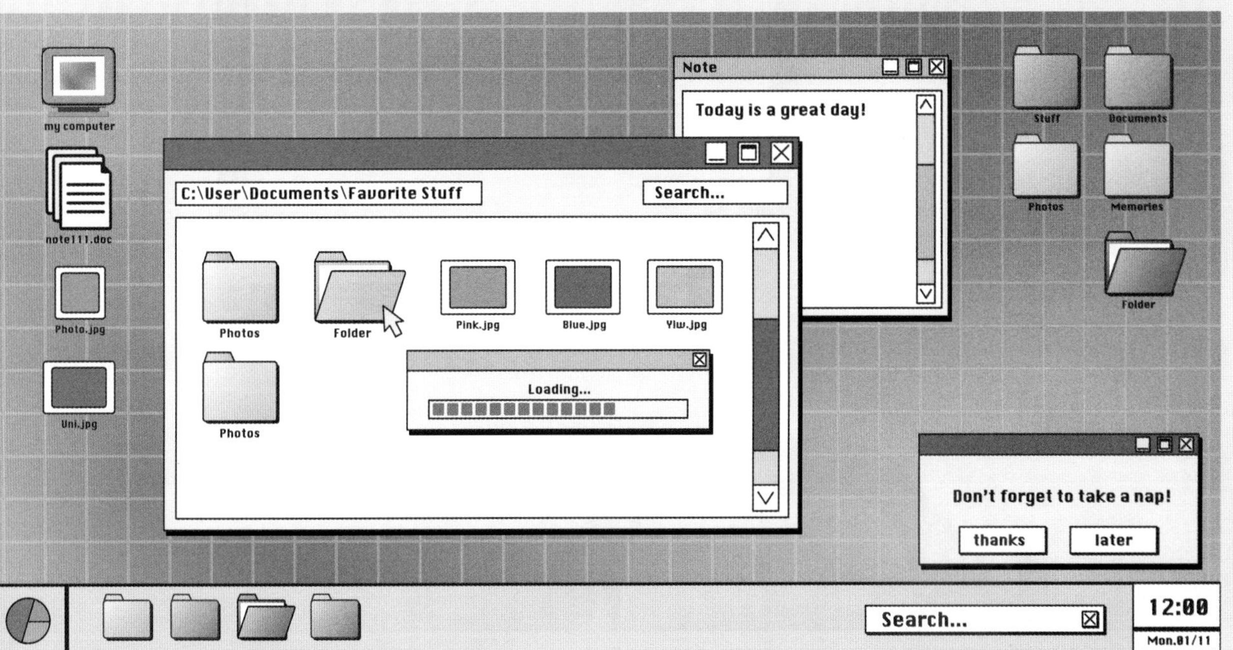

Figure 4.2.1 A typical computer operating system.

The operating system controls access to the computer's hardware, including internal components such as the processor, main memory and secondary storage, as well as external devices such as the keyboard, mouse and printer.

The operating system provides a platform for all other software on the computer to run, and file management tools that provide access to your files. It comes with **utility software** such as antivirus which keeps the computer secure and in working order. However, it is **application software** that allows the person using the computer to do a task; for example, a web browser or a word processor. Application software is installed by the user and is not part of the operating system. You may have come across this term when downloading software for your phone, which is often called an **app** – this is short for application software!

Tip

If you have been following the course throughout earlier Stages, you will have learned about application and system software in Stage 7.

Figure 4.2.2 Typical operating system apps.

The computer system has a finite amount of resources, such as memory and processor time, and the operating system shares these resources between the software that is running. Requests from software to use hardware devices, for example, when you press 'print' in a word processing program, are also dealt with by the operating system. The operating system uses small pieces of software called **drivers**, which communicate with a hardware device such as a printer so that the document prints out correctly.

Workbook page 47: Complete Task A, '**Which tasks are performed by the operating system?**'.

Build the troubleshooter

Problems with a computer can often be resolved by using tools provided by the operating system. Here are some of the tasks that are handled by the operating system:

- It allows software to control the hardware.
- It manages files.
- It allocates the computer's resources, for example memory.

Discuss 3

Can you think of any computer problems you might have which would relate to these tasks? For example, a printer not working, not being able to find a file or the computer running slowly. How would you resolve each of the problems?

Workbook page 47: Complete Task B, '**Troubleshooter problems**'.

Build 2:

Add some more questions to your troubleshooter tool that are related to the operating system and the tasks it performs.

Workbook page 48: Complete the '**Reflection**' task.

Chapter 4.3 Utility programs

What do we already know?

- Utility software keeps the computer secure and in working order, for example antivirus software

Key terms

Compression – in some cases reducing the amount of storage space a file requires

Malware – **mal**icious soft**ware**. Any software that intends to cause harm to a computer, for example a virus

What is a utility program?

Discuss 4

What do you think a utility program is? What different types can you name?

A utility program is a small piece of software that keeps the computer secure and in working order. Utility programs usually perform a single very specific task.

File manager – the operating system keeps track of all the data and files stored in secondary storage, and it displays the files in an organised way so that you can find them easily. Usually, files are organised into named folders, and each type of file is displayed with its own icon.

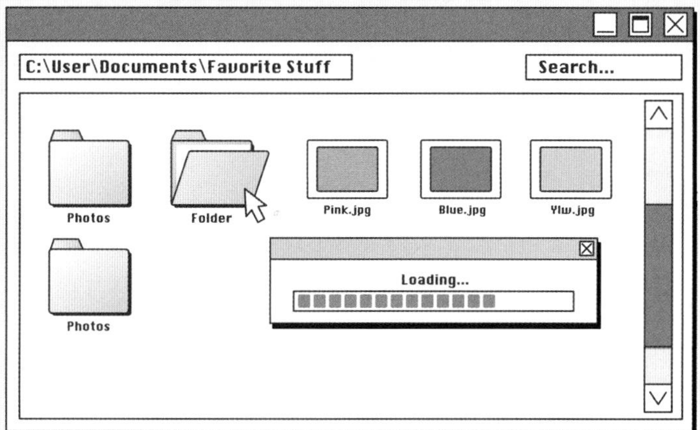

Figure 4.3.1 A user organising their files and folders.

Backup – a backup program can back up the data on your computer by making a copy of it somewhere else, for example on a portable USB drive. If there is a problem with the computer, the data can then be retrieved from the backup.

Compression – some types of file, such as images and videos, take up a lot of storage space. The operating system can compress files, in some cases significantly reducing the amount of storage space a file requires.

Anti-malware – prevents malicious software or '**malware**' from causing harm to your computer by detecting and removing it. The software runs in the background to detect malware, but can also be used to scan a specific document, such as an email attachment. Anti-malware software relies on regular updates, as new viruses are constantly being created.

Figure 4.3.2 Anti-malware software scanning a computer.

Workbook page 49: Complete Task A, '**Purpose of utility programs**'.

Anti-malware software on a network

Figure 4.3.3 An example of ransomware locking a computer.

Although it is important to protect your own computer from viruses, it is even more important to protect computers that are part of a network, for example in a school, hospital or business.

In 2017, the UK's state healthcare system (called the 'NHS') was targeted by a virus called 'WannaCry', which encrypted data and demanded a ransom. This meant that doctors could not access patient records, and many people had appointments or even surgery cancelled. The virus spread to thousands of computers across the NHS network, and probably originated from one person opening an infected email attachment on an old computer that had not been updated with the latest security protection.

Antivirus software is a very important security tool on a network because it:

- scans the network and blocks malicious software from circulating
- is kept up to date centrally by the organisation's IT support, meaning individual users don't need to worry about updates
- prevents a type of malware called 'spyware' gathering confidential data from within the network and leaking it.

Workbook page 49: Complete Task B, '**Advice from a technician**'.

Build 3:

Add some more questions to your troubleshooter tool which relate to utility software. Follow the same process as you did during the previous lesson.

- Think of computer problems which relates to utility software, e.g. "my computer has a virus" or "my printer isn't working".
- Do you need to ask any more information to be able to offer some advice? If so, what would be the next question you would ask?
- Do you know how to resolve the problem? If so, write down the advice. If not, research or ask a classmate.

Workbook page 50: Complete the '**Reflection**' task.

Chapter 4.4 Unauthorised access

What do we already know?

- Data is broken down into packets, which are transmitted across a network as 'network traffic'
- The URL of a website (e.g. https://www.example.com) has a corresponding IP address (e.g. 192.168.3.10)

Key terms

File access permissions – restrict access to files and folders on a network to only the people who need to see them

Firewall – provides a layer of protection between two networks, preventing threats from entering, and sensitive information from leaving

Port – a number assigned to each type of network traffic going in or out of a firewall

What is a firewall?

The term firewall did originally refer to an actual fire! Large buildings such as apartment blocks often have fire resistant 'firewalls' built in, so that if a fire starts it can be contained in one area of the building, leaving time for people to be evacuated.

A computer firewall works in the same way, except there is no real fire involved. A **firewall** provides a layer of protection between two networks, so that threats can be prevented from entering, and sensitive information can be contained within the network.

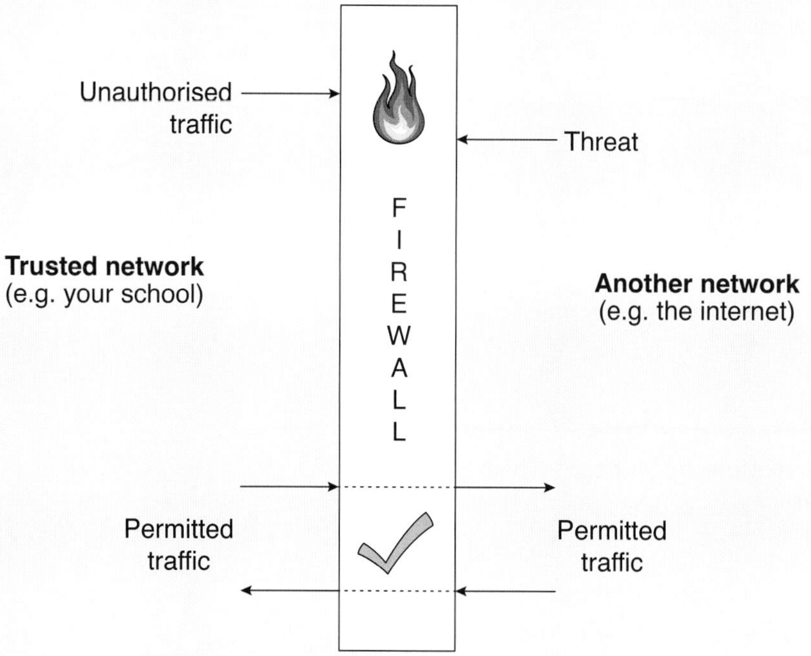

Figure 4.4.1 A diagram of a firewall.

Figure 4.4.2 Two students simulating traffic attempting to access a network.

Each type of traffic going in and out of the firewall uses a **port**, which is a number assigned to each type of network traffic going in or out of the firewall. Different types of network traffic have different default ports; for example, when you look at a website via HTTPS this is usually via port 443, but a different port number can also be specified.

Tip

If your school has a filtering system and you have tried to access a site that is not permitted by the school, you have probably encountered a firewall.

Investigate 1

You are going to work in a group to simulate different traffic coming in and out of a trusted network via a firewall and investigate whether it will be allowed or blocked.

Your teacher will give you the list of rules for the firewall. Fill in the table in Workbook pages 51 and 52: Task A, 'Simulate a firewall' as you go.

File access permissions

Firewalls can protect the network from threats coming in from outside. However, they cannot protect the network against threats that originate inside the network.

File access permissions restrict access to files and folders on a network to only the people who *need* to see them or edit them. They can apply to individual documents, folders or even whole drives of a computer.

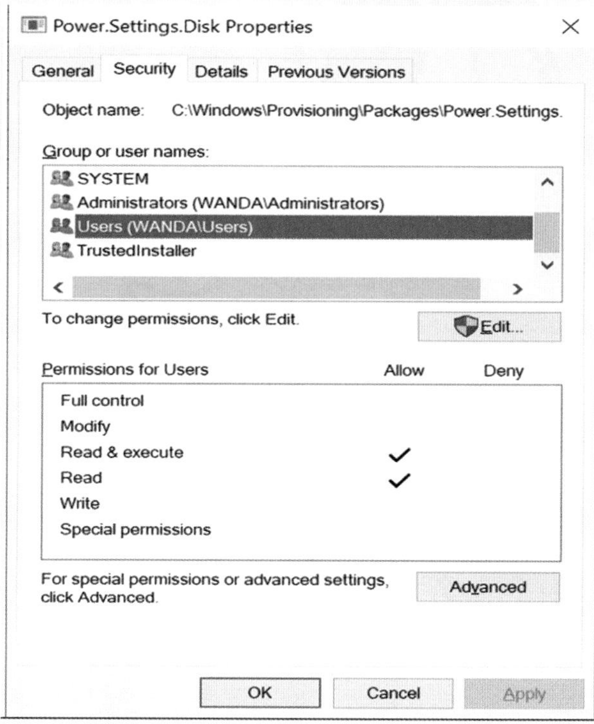

This is a screenshot of the security settings for a file that is part of the operating system on a person's computer. The user has permission to read (see what is inside) and execute (run) this file. However, they do not have permission to modify (change) or write (add to) the file.

Network file access permissions work in the same way. Staff at your school probably have access to read, write and modify files and directories on your school network that you cannot even see. For example, your class teacher may need read access for medical records of students in case someone falls ill in class, but they would not have write access as they do not need to change the data. Staff who deal with medical issues in school would have access to write and modify the data.

Sometimes file access permissions are set incorrectly – a user may not be able to access a file that they think they should have access to. In this case, the usual solution is to contact the network administrator who will investigate the permissions and add additional permissions for that user if they are needed.

Protecting a network from threats

Discuss 5

Think about the following scenario:

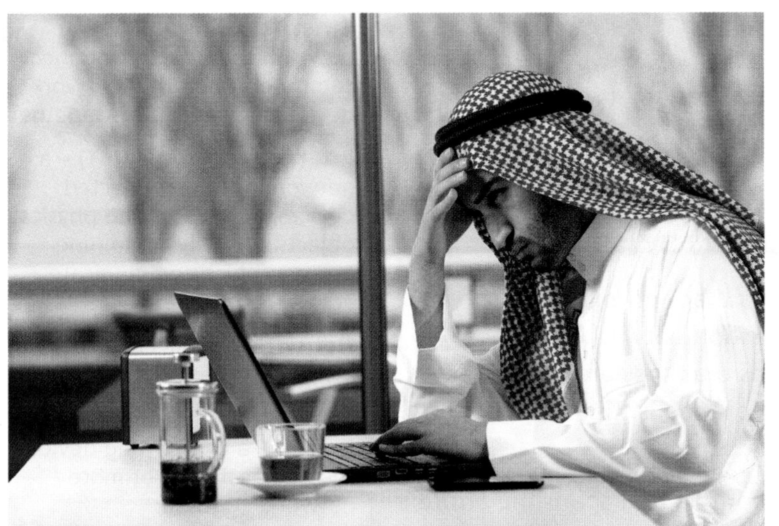

Figure 4.4.2 Faisal's dilemma. A software engineer has sent data to an unknown recipient on the internet.

Faisal works as a software engineer for a large company, which sells software to other businesses. Faisal receives an email from the head of the company – he is at a conference and wants Faisal to immediately send across a document containing the details of all orders in the city where the conference is being held. Not wanting to keep the head of the company waiting, Faisal immediately sends the document to the email address he was given. Later, it turns out that the email request was not genuine, and Faisal has sent the data to an unknown recipient on the internet.

Read the scenario and then answer the questions in the Workbook.

Workbook page 53: Complete Task B '**Keeping data safe inside a network**'.

Build 4:

Add some more questions to your troubleshooter tool, which relate to firewalls and file access permissions. For example, you might ask whether they are having trouble accessing a particular website.

Workbook page 53: Complete the '**Reflection**' task.

Chapter 4.5 Network connections and the IoT

What do we already know?

- Networks contain devices such as routers and Wi-Fi access points
- Data can be transferred wirelessly across a network
- Encryption keeps data secure during transmission

Wired and wireless networks

A **network** is a collection of computers that are connected together to exchange data. The connection between the computers may be **wired**, which means that they are connected together with cables, or **wireless**, which means that they connect and communicate using radio signals.

The internet is a huge network of computers that spans the entire world. Huge undersea fibre-optic cables provide a connection between continents, allowing signals to travel at the speed of light.

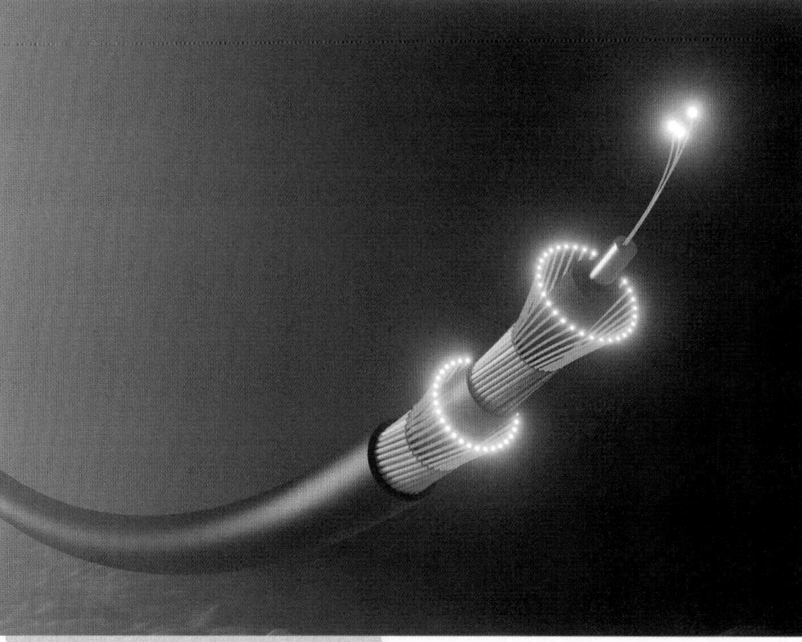

Figure 4.5.1 A fibre-optic cable that transmits data as pulses of light.

Key terms

Ethernet cable – a type of network cable used to connect computers and other network devices such as routers together

Internet of Things (IoT) – a network of interconnected devices, appliances and physical objects, typically containing sensors, which communicate across the internet

Network – a collection of computers that are connected together to exchange data

Router – a networking device that connects two or more networks together

Wired network – computers and network devices connected using physical cables such as ethernet cables

Wireless network – computers and network devices that connect and communicate via radio signals

Fibre-optic cables are also laid across the country, underneath the roads, so that each building can be connected to the internet. Once the building is connected, smaller cables called **ethernet** cables are laid throughout the building, and these can be used to connect individual devices such as a router or a desktop computer. Cabling a whole building can be very expensive, but ethernet cables provide a fast connection to all devices capable of being plugged into the network.

Figure 4.5.2 An ethernet cable.

A device called a wireless **router** can be connected to the network via a cable. The router will broadcast a radio signal, and other devices such as laptops and tablets can then join the network wirelessly. Wireless connections are slower than wired connections because data cannot be transmitted as quickly via radio signal. Wireless devices can be used anywhere in range of the router, although the strength of signal can vary in different areas of the building.

Figure 4.5.3 A wireless router.

It is extremely important that a wireless network is properly secured. Modern routers encrypt their traffic so that data being transmitted cannot be intercepted. However, if a secure password is not used to join the network, or if the password is freely advertised, for example in a cafe, anyone can access the network without needing to be physically inside the building. This makes wireless networks a much more tempting target for hackers.

Workbook page 55: Complete Task A '**Advantages and disadvantages of wired and wireless networks**'.

Network connected devices

Providing a device with a method of connecting to the internet is becoming increasingly common. The **Internet of Things** or **IoT** is a network of interconnected devices, appliances and physical objects, typically containing sensors, which communicate across the internet.

Examples of IoT devices include smart speakers, doorbell cameras, fitness trackers and healthcare devices.

Figure 4.5.4 A smart speaker.

Figure 4.5.5 A doorbell camera.

Figure 4.5.6 A fitness tracker.

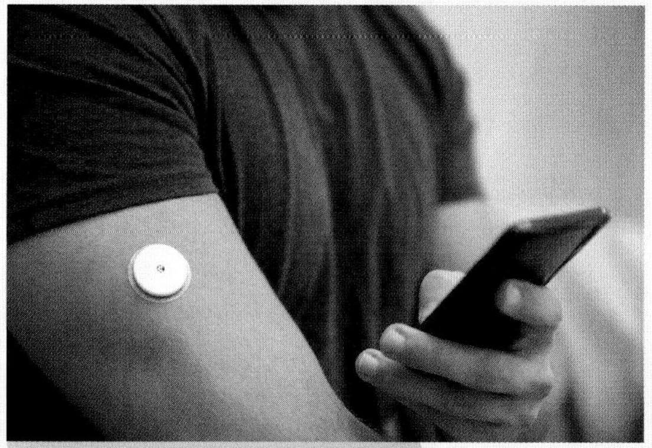

Figure 4.5.7 A healthcare device.

Investigate 2

In groups, research a specific IoT device. Create a two-slide presentation explaining the benefits of the device, and the risks associated with it being connected to the internet.

Build 5:

Add some more questions to your troubleshooter tool, which relate to network connections and the Internet of Things.

Workbook page 56: Complete the '**Reflection**' task.

Troubleshooter

What do we already know?

- You have covered memory, the operating system, utility programs, unauthorised access, network connections and the Internet of Things
- You have created a troubleshooter flowchart to diagnose and offer advice on computer problems

Test your troubleshooter

By now, you will have created a substantial troubleshooting tool that can be used to diagnose and solve computer problems.

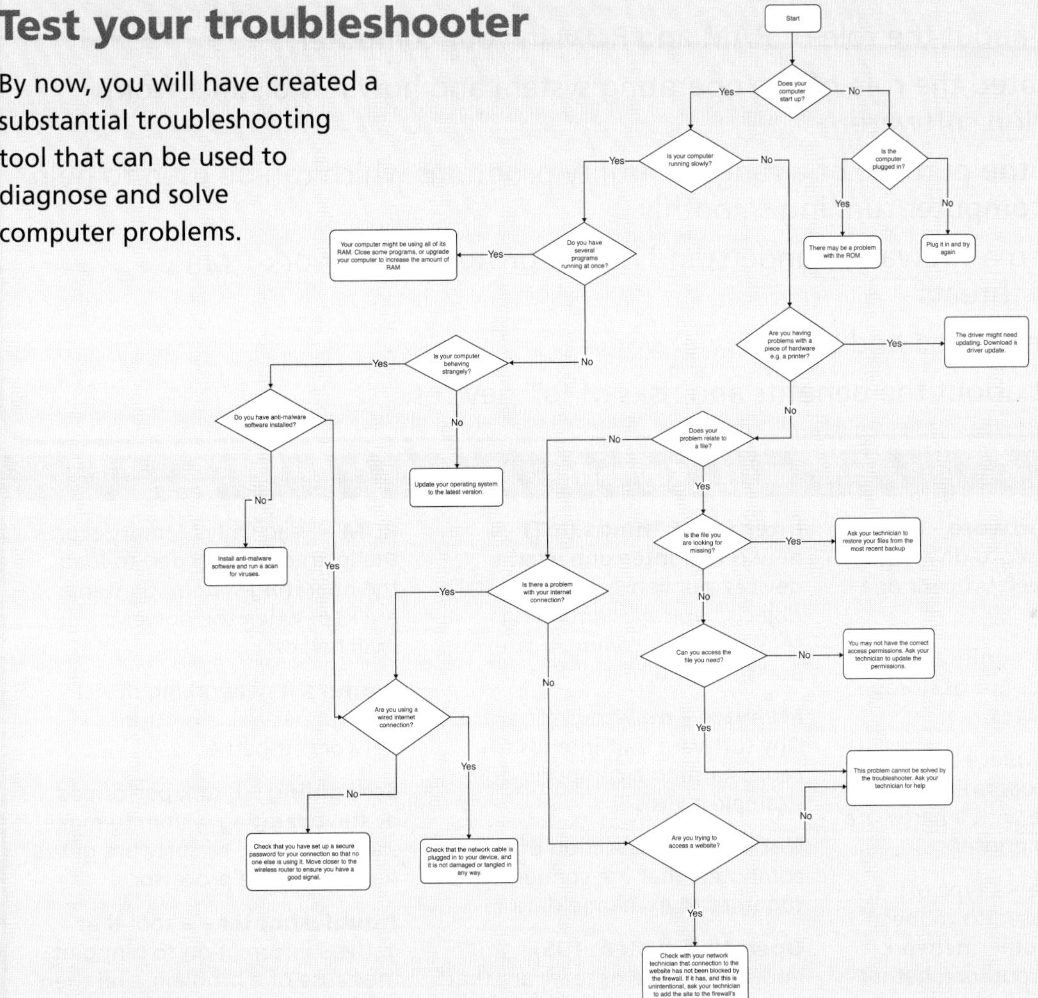

Role play 2

In pairs, you will work together to test the troubleshooting tool you have been putting together throughout this project. Your teacher will give you some scenarios of computer problems. Take it in turns to play the role of the computer user and the computer technician and use your troubleshooting tool to provide advice on how to fix the user's problem. Note down your findings in your Workbook.

Workbook page 57: Complete Task A, '**Test the troubleshooter**'.

Workbook page 58: Complete the '**Reflection**' task.

Well done! **You have completed Chapter 4, 'How computers work'.**

In this chapter you:

- ☑ created a troubleshooting tool that could find and offer advice about how to solve computer problems
- ☑ learned about the role of RAM and ROM in your computer
- ☑ investigated the role of the operating system and how it is distinct from application software
- ☑ learned the purpose of a range of utility programs which can be used to help keep a computer running smoothly
- ☑ simulated a firewall to understand how it protects a network from external threats
- ☑ compared wired and wireless networks
- ☑ thought about the benefits and risks of IoT devices.

Key terms

Application software – allows the computer user to do a task, for example a web browser or a word processor

Compression – significantly reducing the amount of storage space a file requires

Driver – a small piece of software that allows the operating system to communicate with a hardware device such as a printer

Ethernet cable – a type of network cable used to connect computers and other network devices such as routers together

File access permissions – restrict access to files and folders on a network to only the people who need to see them

Firewall – provides a layer of protection between two networks, preventing threats from entering, and sensitive information from leaving

Internet of Things (IoT) – a network of interconnected devices, appliances and physical objects, typically containing sensors, which communicate across the internet

Malware – **mal**icious soft**ware**. Any software that intends to cause harm to a computer, for example a virus

Network – a collection of computers that are connected together to exchange data

Operating system (OS) – an important piece of software that manages all other software and hardware devices

Port – a number assigned to each type of network traffic going in or out of a firewall

RAM – Random Access Memory, used to store instructions and data the computer is currently working with. Contents are lost when the power is switched off

ROM – Read Only Memory, stores the instructions needed to load the operating system. Contents are kept when the power is switched off

Router – a networking device that connects two or more networks together

Scheduling – a task performed by the operating system to make sure each piece of software gets a turn to use the processor

Troubleshooter – a tool that gathers information to pinpoint the cause of a problem, and then offers advice on how to fix it

Utility software – keeps the computer secure and in working order, for example antivirus software

Wired network – computers and network devices connected using physical cables such as ethernet cables

Wireless network – computers and network devices that connect and communicate via radio signals

Reflect: What can you do now that you couldn't do before?

Chapter 5 Create with code 2

Project: Animal quiz

In this chapter, you will:

- recap different types of data used in a program – integer, real, Boolean, string
- use these data types in a text-based program
- learn how to make decisions (if/elif/else) in a text-based program
- create truth tables for the logic gates AND, OR and NOT
- design and program algorithms using AND, OR and NOT logic.

End of chapter project: Animal quiz

In this chapter, you will create a multiple-choice animal quiz program that you can play with your friends.

- Use the starter code to begin your quiz.
- Add at least four questions, with multiple choice answers.
- Each question should require a logical operator – `and`, `or` or `not` to check whether the answer is correct
- Add points to the player's score each time they get a question correct. You can decide how many points to award for each correct answer, and whether you would like to deduct points for giving a wrong answer.

```
Welcome to the quiz!
Which two animals have wings?
A - Bat
B - Parrot
C - Rhinoceros
D - Tiger
Enter A, B, C or D for the first animal: A
Enter A, B, C or D for the second animal: C
Oh no, you got it wrong :(
Give one continent where bears are a native species
A - Europe
B - Africa
C - Asia
D - Australia
Enter A, B, C or D: C
You know a lot about animals!
Which of the following animals is NOT a herbivore?
A - Snail
B - Elephant
C - Horse
D - Rabbit
Enter A, B, C or D: B
Whoops, that wasn't right
Congratulations! Your score was 1
```

Figure 5.0.1 A text-based animal quiz.

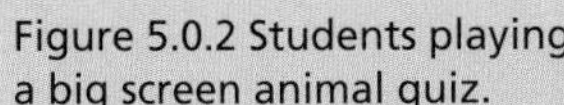
Figure 5.0.2 Students playing a big screen animal quiz.

Chapter 5.1 Data types

What do we already know?

- Programs use variables to store data
- Data can have different types, such as integer, real number or string
- A program can let the user input data and output data to the screen
- You can concatenate (join) two strings together

Key terms

Boolean – a type of data that can have one of two possible values: true or false

Cast – change the data type of a piece of data

Data types

Computer programs use different types of data, including:

- Integers – whole numbers
- Real numbers – numbers with fractional parts
- Strings – a mixture of one or more letters, numbers and characters.

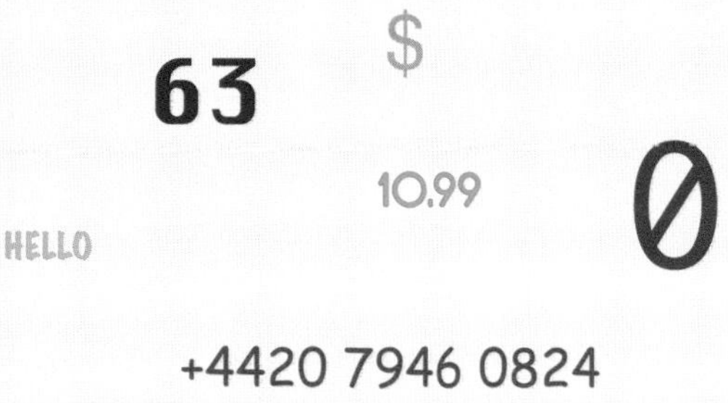

63

$

10.99

0

HELLO

+4420 7946 0824

Figure 5.1.1 Examples of different types of data.

Discuss 1

Look at the examples of data given in the image above. Discuss with a partner and decide whether each piece of data would be stored as an integer, a real number or a string.

There is another type of data called **Boolean**, which can have one of two values – it is either true or false. This type of data is very useful when you want to make a decision in a program.

Tip

You learned about Boolean logic in Stage 7 when you created a recommendation system.

Python interprets the data type of a variable based on how the data is presented in the program. It is important to remember that *any data within quotation marks is a string*. Boolean values must not use quotes, and the first letter must be uppercase.

Data type	Example
Integer	`age = 14`
Real number (float)	`price = 23.99`
String	`name = "Jatinder"` `currency = "$"`
Boolean	`raining = True` `finished = False`

Tip

Python uses the word 'float' to refer to real numbers. This is short for 'floating point number' and refers to the format in which computers store numbers with fractional parts, for example 1.5.

Mathematical operators

You can use mathematical operators to perform calculations in Python, just as you would in a Mathematics lesson. The addition (+), subtraction (-), multiplication (*) and division (/) operators all work in exactly the same way. Here is an example of multiplication:

```
price = 10
how_many = 2
total = price * how_many
print(total)
```

This code would output 20.

Data input

To allow the user to input data into a program in Python, use the `input()` function. You could replace the number 2 in the previous program with an input to allow the user to type the quantity they wish to buy:

```
how_many = input("How many would you like to buy? ")
```

Investigate 1

Predict what the output of this code will be if the user types in 2 as the input:

```
price = 10
how_many = input("How many would you like to
buy? ")
total = price * how_many
print("The total price is " + total)
```

Casting

The input function *always* returns a string. If you want to type in numerical data to use a calculation, you need to **cast** (change) it to a different data type. If you forget, you will either get an error, or some very unexpected results!

To cast data to a different data type, add the name of the data type you want – `int()`, `float()` or `str()` – with brackets around the data you want to cast. The code to perform the calculation correctly looks like this – the variable `how_many` is cast to an integer, then used in the calculation, and then the variable `total` is cast back to a string so that it can be concatenated with the printed information.

```
price = 10
how_many = input("How many would you like to buy? ")
how_many = int(how_many)
total = price * how_many
print("The total price is " + str(total))
```

Workbook page 60: Complete Task A, '**What type of data?**'.

Chatbot

To practise using input, output and concatenation in a program, you are going to create a small chatbot. The chatbot will ask you questions, and then reply, using your reply as part of its answer. Here is the code for an example question:

```
sport = input("What is your favourite sport? ")
print("That's cool, I like " + sport + " too")
```

Here is the output from this code, if the user types in 'tennis':

```
What is your favourite sport?
> tennis
That's cool, I like tennis too
```

Tip

The > at the start of the line in this example indicates that the user has typed an input.

Workbook page 61: Complete Task B, '**Chatbot questions**'.

Build 1:

Write a program to create a simple chatbot that can ask the questions you have planned, and then use the input you typed in the reply.

Workbook page 61: Complete the '**Reflection**' task.

Chapter 5.2 Pseudocode

What do we already know?

- You can plan the logic of a program using a flowchart
- Mathematics: How to calculate a percentage increase or decrease using a decimal multiplier

Key terms

Program logic – how the design of the program is implemented

Pseudocode – a method of planning a program using statements that have a clear and precise meaning, but are not written in any particular programming language

Syntax – the structure of a statement in a programming language

What is pseudocode?

When you have previously planned a program, you may have used a flowchart to help you to translate between what you want the program to do and the **program logic**, which is the way the program is implemented.

In this lesson, you will learn another way of planning a program. **Pseudocode** is a method of planning a program using statements that have a clear and precise meaning, but are not written in any particular programming language.

Planning a program

Look at the following example of a plan for a program that asks the user to type in two numbers and then adds them together. The same program has been planned both as a flowchart and using pseudocode.

Discuss 2

What are the similarities and differences between the two ways of planning a program: using a flowchart and using pseudocode?

Flowchart

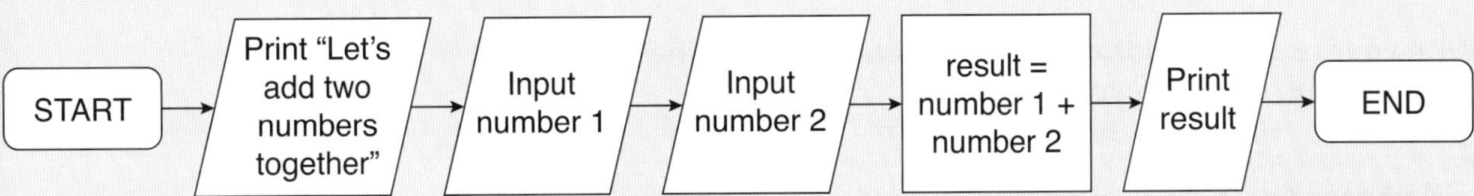

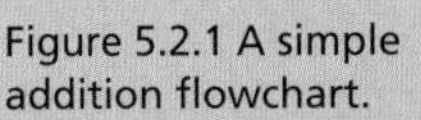
Figure 5.2.1 A simple addition flowchart.

Pseudocode

```
PRINT "Let's add two numbers together"
number1 = INPUT number 1
number2 = INPUT number 2
result = number1 + number2
PRINT "The result is " + result
```

Workbook page 62: Complete Task A, '**Similarities and differences**'.

Now you will practise translating a flowchart into pseudocode.

Workbook page 61: Complete Task B, '**Flowchart to pseudocode**'.

Discuss 3

Compare your answer to Workbook, Task B with a partner. Are they the same? Do they both have clear and precise instructions?

The format of pseudocode

You have probably noticed that pseudocode looks a lot like Python code, so you might wonder what the point of it is when you could just write directly in code. The main reason to use pseudocode is that you can write a program without having to remember the exact **syntax**, that is, the format of the statement in Python. There are no rules for pseudocode because it is not a programming language, and it can be typed or written on paper. For example, the following four statements would all be acceptable in pseudocode:

```
number1 = INPUT number 1
INPUT an integer and STORE as number1
number1 = input a number
number1 -> type in an integer
```

However, none of those statements would be valid Python code. As long as the pseudocode instructions are short, clear and precise, the meaning is clear, and the instructions can later be translated into valid Python code:

```
number1 = int(input("Type in an integer"))
```

With your teacher, decide on some pseudocode guidelines and then write these in your Workbook.

Workbook page 62: Complete Task C, '**Pseudocode guidelines**'.

Pseudocode to code

You are going to plan a shopping helper program using pseudocode. The program should allow you to type in the price of an item and the % discount in a sale. It should then calculate the price you will pay when the discount has been applied. You can do this using the decimal multiplier method for calculating percentage increases and decreases.

To find the decimal multiplier for a decrease, first take away the % decrease from 100%. For an increase, add the % increase to 100.

So, if there is a 20% discount:
100% - 20% = 80%

Then, calculate 80% as a decimal:
80 / 100 = 0.8

Tip

You can also find the decimal without doing any calculations, just add 0. in front of your percentage, for example 0.80

Design 1

Use a word processor or text editor program to write some pseudocode for a shopping helper program. Here is an example which shows what might happen when the program is running:

```
>>> Hello, what would you like to buy?
scarf
>>> Please enter the price of the scarf
10.99
>>> What is the % discount?
20
>>> A scarf with a 20% discount costs 8.79
```

Build 2:

Swap pseudocode with a partner and use their pseudocode to implement the program in Python.

Workbook page 63: Complete the '**Reflection**' task.

Chapter 5.3 IF, ELIF and ELSE

What do we already know?

- How to follow and use selection statements in flowcharts

Key terms

Condition – a test in a program that evaluates to a Boolean value – either true or false

Comparison operator – an operator that allows you to compare two values, for example to check whether they are equal, or one is greater than the other

Flow of control – the order in which the statements in a program are executed

Selection – when a program executes different code based on a condition

Selection

You have seen and used **selection** statements before.

Scratch

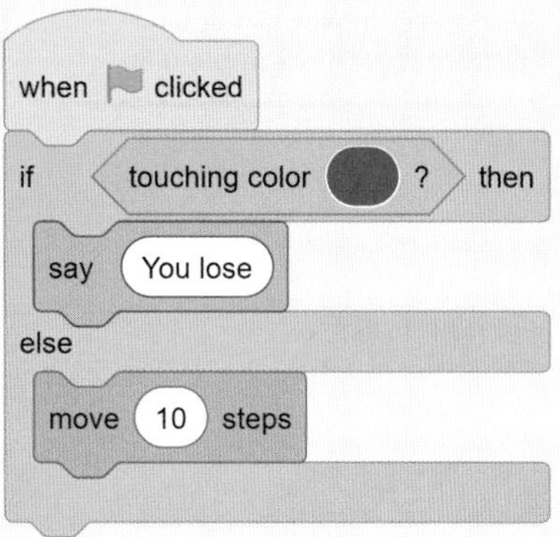

Figure 5.3.1 A Scratch program that uses selection.

Flowcharts

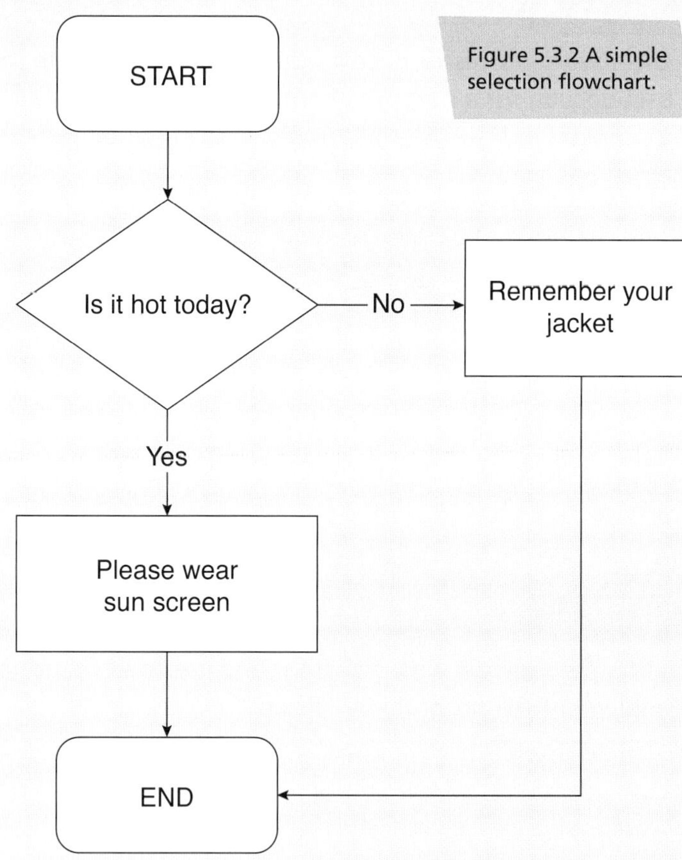

Figure 5.3.2 A simple selection flowchart.

A **condition** is a statement in a program that evaluates to either true or false. Selection causes different code to be executed, or carried out, depending on the result of the condition. Can you identify the condition in each of the examples above?

Workbook page 64: Complete Task A, '**Write some conditions**'.

Comparison operators

In Python, you will need to use **comparison operators** in your conditions so that you can compare values and make decisions. You have seen and used all of these operators before, but here is how they are written in Python.

==	Equal to	!=	Not equal to
>=	Greater than or equal to	<=	Less than or equal to
>	Greater than	<	Less than

Workbook page 64: Complete Task B, '**Evaluate the conditions**'.

Selection in Python

In Python, a selection statement looks like this:

```
if condition:
  # Code runs if the condition above is true
else:
  # Code runs if all previous conditions are false
```

When you started your chatbot program during the first lesson, your chatbot was fairly limited because it could only make the same comment about what you typed in every time you ran the program. Using a selection statement, you can make your bot reply differently if you add a condition that includes the value typed in by the user:

```
drink = input("What is your favourite drink? ")
if drink == "water":
  print("That's a really healthy choice")
else:
  print("That sounds nice")
```

If the user types water as their favourite drink, the condition [code] drink == "water"[code/] is true. The indented lines of code after the condition will execute:

```
What is your favourite drink?
> water
That's a really healthy choice
```

If the user types in anything else, the condition will be false, and so the indented lines of code after the `else` statement will execute. Python is case-sensitive, so the user's input must match the condition exactly – even typing the same word in capitals will mean that the condition is false.

```
What is your favourite drink?
> WATER
That sounds nice
```

Tip

The **flow of control** is the order in which the statements in a program are executed. Statements are executed one after another in turn *unless* the flow of control is altered. A selection statement causes the program to evaluate a condition and only execute some lines of code if the associated condition is true.

Build 3:

Use the example on page 80 to edit the questions in your chatbot program. For each question, the chatbot should test a condition and give a different response depending on what the user types.

Elif

Sometimes, you may want to ask a question and test more than one condition when giving a response. Python allows you to write as many conditions as you like within a selection statement. The first one is written as `if` and each subsequent condition is written as `elif`. Here is how the statement works:

- Each condition is tested in turn. If the condition is true, the indented code will be executed.
- As soon as *any* condition has been matched and its code executed, the flow of control will skip *all* of the rest of the conditions and move to the next program statement.
- If none of the conditions are true, and there is an `else`, the indented code for `else` will be executed.

Here is an example of a selection statement with an additional condition:

```
age = int(input("How old are you? "))
if age >= 40:
  print("You're really old!")
elif age > 18:
  print("You're an adult")
else:
  print("You are probably at school")
```

If the user types in their age as 90, the first condition will be tested and found to be true, so they will receive the message "You're really old!".

If the user types in their age as 30, the first condition will be tested, but since 30 >= 40 is false, the program moves to the next condition. 30 > 18 is true, so they will receive the message "You're an adult".

Tip

Remember, you can have as many `elif` conditions as you like, but the first condition must always be an `if` and the `else` must always be last as it matches anything not previously tested.

Build 4:

Add another question to your chatbot that uses an `elif` statement. This can be a new question, or you can modify an existing question if you prefer.

Workbook page 64: Complete the '**Reflection**' task.

Chapter 5.4 AND, OR, NOT

What do we already know?

- Computers are made up of logic gates that are represented by Boolean logic
- How logic gates work, including AND, OR and NOT
- How to write Python code for a selection statement

Key terms

Logic gate – a circuit inside a computer that allows Boolean logic to be applied to one or more inputs

Truth table – a diagram showing all possible combinations of inputs and outputs from a Boolean expression

Boolean logic

Logic gates are circuits inside a computer that are used to apply Boolean logic to one or more inputs. You have studied AND, OR and NOT gates before in Stage 7.

Workbook page 66: Complete Task A, '**Recap logic gates**'.

Truth tables

A **truth table** is a diagram that shows all possible combinations of inputs and outputs from a logic statement. 0 is used to represent False and 1 is used to represent True.

To create a truth table:

- Work out all the different possible combinations of input and write each one in a row of the table. There is only one input for a NOT gate so there are only two possibilities: 1 or 0.

Input	Output
1	
0	

- Create the logic gate in the logic gate simulator (a link will be provided by your teacher). Use a switch for each input, and a light bulb to show the output.

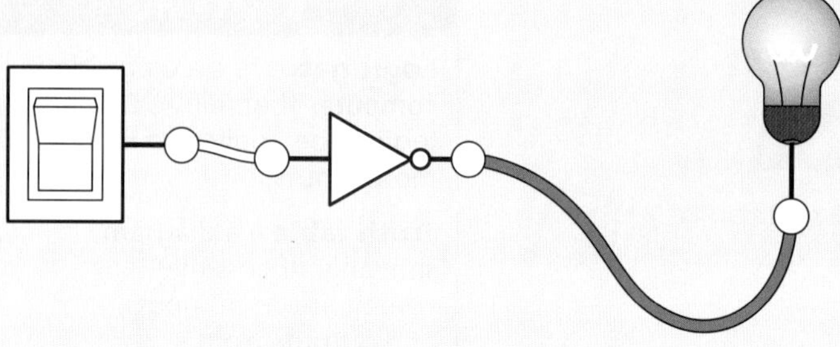

Figure 5.4.1 A switch connected to a light bulb via a NOT gate.

- For each row in the table, set the correct input(s) in your simulator and write down the output.

Input	Output
1	0
0	1

Workbook page 66: Complete Task B, '**Complete the truth tables**'.

Why would you use a truth table?

Logic can be found in all sorts of everyday situations. For example, security lights installed on buildings come on when it is dark. Here is a truth table for a security light:

Sun?	Light on?
0	1
1	0

When the sun is not shining (0), the light comes on (1), and when the sun *is* shining (1) the light is off (0). This is the same as the truth table for the NOT gate.

Discuss 4

For each of the following scenarios, what are the inputs, and which logic gate is represented by the truth table?

- A barrier to exit a car park that will lift when a car is present and a ticket is inserted
- A restaurant that does not allow people in if they are wearing trainers
- A vending machine that dispenses a drink if money has been inserted and a button has been pressed
- A fridge that sounds an alarm if the door is left open or if the temperature goes above 8 °C

Boolean logic in Python

Figure 5.4.2 A student entering a username and password.

You have used **logical operators** in programs before. In Python the operators are written as words in lowercase.

Operator	Example
and	if a and b:
or	if a or b:
not	if not a:

Build 5:

Write a Python program that asks for a username and password, and uses a logical operator to check whether the user is allowed in. Here is a plan in pseudocode:

```
INPUT username
INPUT password
IF username EQUALS "zoya" AND password
EQUALS "apple32"
  PRINT "You are logged in"
ELSE
  PRINT "Incorrect username or password"
```

Test that Zoya sees a message saying that she has logged in if she inputs the correct username and password.

Build 6:

Add another valid account to your program with the username "admin" and password "secret", *without* adding an additional if or elif statement.

Tip

You will need to combine two logical operators in your condition.

Workbook page 67: Complete the '**Reflection**' task.

Chapter 5.5 Design and build a quiz program

What do we already know?

- Follow and describe logic AND, OR, NOT
- How to plan a program using pseudocode

Key terms

Indentation – positioning code further in from the left

Logical operator – AND, OR or NOT

Sequence – statements in code that execute in the order in which they are written

Selection in pseudocode

The pseudocode statements you used previously were part of a **sequence**, which means that the code is executed in the order in which it is written. You know that selection statements affect the flow of control, because some lines of code will only execute if a condition is met. When you write pseudocode for selection, you need to make clear which statements are part of the selection statement.

Discuss 5

What will be the output from this pseudocode if the score input is 5?

```
INPUT score
IF score > 10
OUTPUT "Excellent score"
OUTPUT "Well done"
```

To ensure that the pseudocode is clear in its meaning, you should use indentation to show which statements are part of a condition and which are not. Here is pseudocode for the same algorithm, where meaning has been made completely clear by using both **indentation** and an `ENDIF` statement to indicate the end of the code inside the condition.

```
INPUT score
IF score > 10
  OUTPUT "Excellent score"
ENDIF
OUTPUT "Well done"
```

The output from this updated version of the pseudocode is completely clear. If the user inputs 15, they will see the extra message because the condition `score > 10` is true.

```
Excellent score
Well done
```

If the user inputs 2, they will see just the final output. This line of code is not indented, so it is not part of the IF statement, and will execute every time the program runs.

```
Well done
```

Animal quiz

Figure 5.5.1 A safari employee planning a quiz.

You are going to write an animal quiz program in Python. The questions will have multiple-choice answers, but each question should require a **logical operator** – `and`, `or` or `not` in Python – to check the answer. Here is an example of a question:

```
OUTPUT "Which two animals have wings?"
OUTPUT "A - Bat"
OUTPUT "B - Parrot"
OUTPUT "C - Rhinoceros"
OUTPUT "D - Tiger"
```

The correct answers to the question are A and B.

Workbook page 68: Complete Task A, '**Finish the pseudocode**'.

Plan your questions

Remember that each question should use a logical operator to check the answer. Here is an example of how you could plan a question using the 'not' operator:

Question	Answer
Type the letter of an animal from this list that is a herbivore: A – Rabbit B – Cat C – Tortoise D - Kangaroo	Not B

Workbook page 69: Complete Task B, '**Plan your quiz questions**'.

Project brief

- Use the starter code to begin your quiz.
- Add at least four questions, with multiple-choice answers.
- Each question should require a logical operator – `and`, `or` or `not` to check whether the answer is correct.
- Add points to the player's score each time they get a question correct. You can decide how many points to award for each correct answer, and whether you would like to deduct points for giving a wrong answer.

Workbook page 69: Complete the '**Reflection**' task.

Chapter 5.6 Showcase your quiz

What do we already know?

- How to write programs using selection statements and Boolean logic in Python

Add a score

In the starter code you were provided, you may have noticed an integer variable at the start:

```
score = 0
```

This variable allows you to keep track of the player's score as they progress through the quiz. For each question they get right, you can add to their score.

```
score = score + 1
```

Figure 5.6.1 A classroom quiz game show.

Build 7:

Finish your quiz program, and make sure you add points to the player's score each time they get a question correct. You can decide how many points to award for each correct answer, and whether you would like to deduct points for any wrong answers!

Showcase your quiz

Showcase

Your teacher will organise you into groups. Play the quiz created by each person in your group and record your score and your feedback notes in the Workbook.

Workbook page 71: Complete Task A, '**Quiz time**'.

Stay safe

Remember that when you use another student's computer to test their work, you must behave responsibly and treat their work with care. Do not make any changes or look at any files other than the quiz you are testing.

Workbook page 72: Complete the '**Reflection**' task.

Congratulations!

Well done! You have completed Chapter 5, 'Create with code'.

In this chapter you:

- ☑ recapped the different types of data
- ☑ created a simple chatbot program
- ☑ learned how to plan a program using pseudocode
- ☑ learned why it is important for your pseudocode to be clear
- ☑ programmed selection statements in python
- ☑ created a truth table for each of the logic gates, AND, OR and NOT
- ☑ researched some facts about animals
- ☑ used your research to create an animal quiz in Python, using logical operators.

Key terms

Boolean – a type of data that can have one of two possible values: true or false

Cast – change the data type of a piece of data

Condition – a test in a program that evaluates to a Boolean value – either true or false

Comparison operator – an operator that allows you to compare two values, for example to check whether they are equal, or one is greater than the other

Flow of control – the order in which the statements in a program are executed

Indentation – positioning code further in from the left

Logical operator – AND, OR or NOT

Logic gate – a circuit inside a computer that allows Boolean logic to be applied to one or more inputs

Program logic – how the design of the program is implemented

Pseudocode – a method of planning a program using statements that have a clear and precise meaning, but are not written in any particular programming language

Selection – when a program executes different code based on a condition

Sequence – statements in code that execute in the order they are written

Syntax – the structure of a statement in a programming language

Truth table – a diagram showing all possible combinations of inputs and outputs from a Boolean expression

Reflect: What can you do now that you couldn't do before?

Chapter 6 Connect the world

Project: Virtual pen pal

In this chapter, you will:

- learn how to count to more than 1000 using your hands
- find out about different sizes of network including PAN, LAN and WAN
- learn how cables allow you to communicate with people all over the world
- write your name without using any letters
- learn about the different ways you can communicate online
- find out how data is compressed
- create a booklet to explain how a message can be instantly transmitted from you to a friend in another country.

End of chapter project: Virtual pen pal

In years gone by, people enjoyed writing letters to each other and sending them in the post. Now lots of people communicate via the Internet, using technology such as instant messages and emails. In this chapter, you will create a booklet to explain the journey a message takes, starting when you type the letters on your computer and ending up with your 'virtual pen pal' on the other side of the world. In this project you will:

- convert numbers between binary and denary
- explain why computers use binary to transmit data
- explain the differences between copper and fibre optic cables
- explain what interference is, and how it affects data being sent via a cable
- explain the difference between PAN, LAN and WAN
- demonstrate how to write a word using ASCII
- convert ASCII codes back to letters and other characters
- describe the benefits and limitations of *at least one* method of online communication
- describe an echo check, and explain why it is used by a computer
- explain the word 'compression'
- use run-length encoding to compress some data
- uncompress some data that has been run-length encoded.

Figure 6.0.1 A student showcasing their work.

Figure 6.0.2 A student guide to messaging a virtual pen pal.

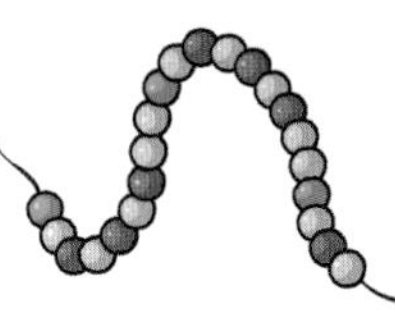

Figure 6.0.3 A set of multicoloured beads.

Binary and denary

What do we already know?

- Describe how numbers are represented in binary

Key terms

Binary – a number system that represents numbers using only two values: 0 and 1

Bit – a single **b**inary dig**it**, either 0 or 1

Denary – the familiar base-10 number system, which uses the digits 0-9

Place value – the value that a digit has because of its position ('place') in the number

Counting in binary

Discuss 1

How can you represent any number between 0 and 1000 just by using your fingers?

Start off with only one hand to make things easier. Use a marker pen or stickers to label each of the fingers on your *right hand*. The thumb starts off as 1, and the value doubles each time, so the next finger is 2, then 4, 8, and the smallest finger is 16.

You can now count up to a maximum of 31 using just this one hand! Each finger has the value written on it, and if the value is visible, you add it to the total. So in this case:

16 + 8 + 4 + 2 + 1 = 31

However, you can represent 32 *different* numbers, because you can also represent zero with no fingers showing.

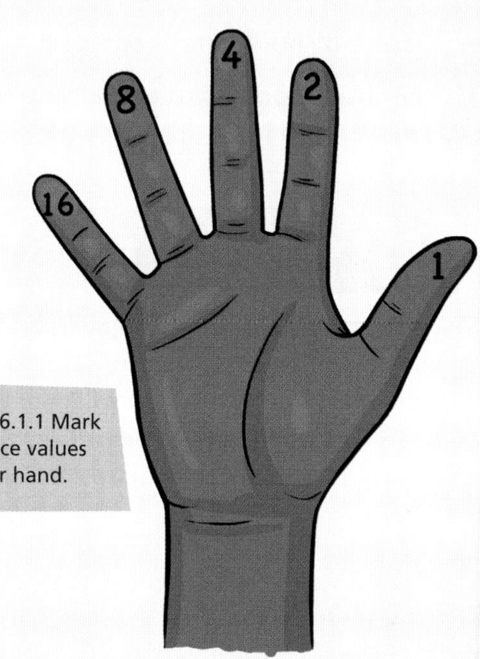

Figure 6.1.1 Mark the place values on your hand.

What number is represented by each of these pictures?

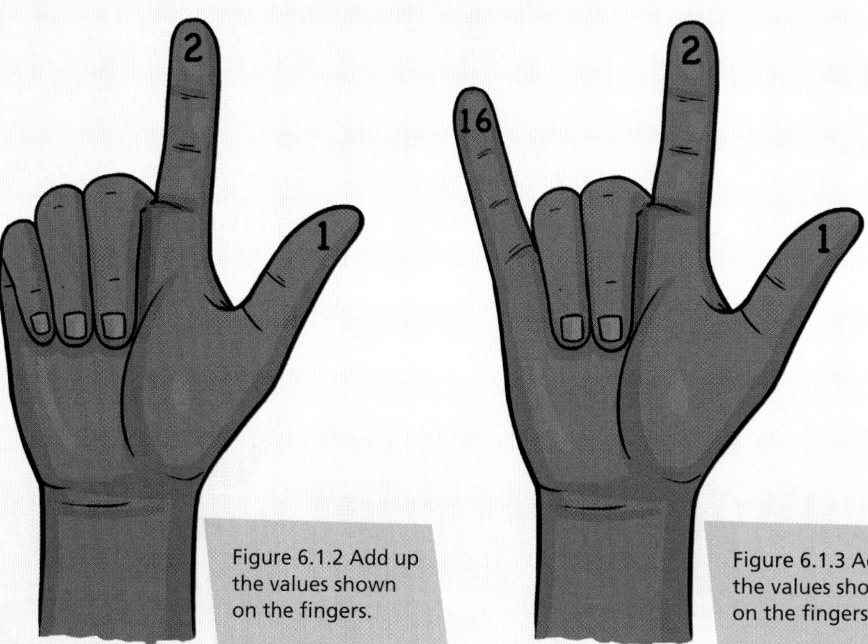

Figure 6.1.2 Add up the values shown on the fingers.

Figure 6.1.3 Add up the values shown on the fingers.

Investigate 1

Pair up with another student and take turns to either show your partner a number using your fingers or work out which number they are showing you.

If you carry on numbering your other hand following the same rule of doubling the value on the finger each time, what is the largest possible number you can represent?

Why binary?

Of course, computers don't have fingers, but they do use the same numbering system, which is called **binary**.

You have already learned about logic gates, which use electrical signals as an input. Computers represent numbers as binary because they can easily switch between two different possibilities – a high voltage (1) or a low voltage (0). Binary is a base-2 number system, which means that the number system only has two digits, 0 or 1.

In this table, the same values as you wrote on your fingers have been written in the top row: these are called **place values**. Below that, a 1 is written if the place value should be added to the total, and a 0 if it is not needed. The number 19 is written as 10011 in binary, which is the same as the number represented by the hand in the picture.

Place value	**16**	**8**	**4**	**2**	**1**
Number	1	0	0	1	1

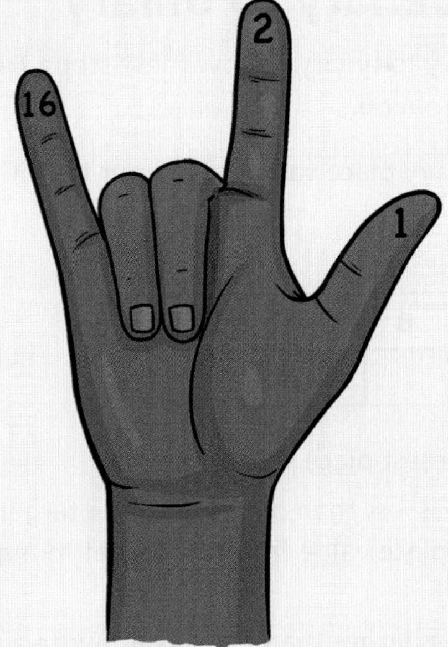

Converting binary to denary

Now that you know how binary works, practise converting some numbers between binary (base-2) and our usual numbering system, which is called **denary** (base-10).

Follow these steps that use the number 01001 as an example.

- Take the binary number and write place values above each digit, starting with 1 above the rightmost digit and doubling the place value each time.

Place value	16	8	4	2	1
Number	0	1	0	0	1

- Add up the place values of any digits that are a 1.

Place value	16	8	4	2	1
Number	0	1	0	0	1

  8 + 1 = 9

So the number 01001 in binary is 9 in denary.

Workbook page 74: Complete Task A, '**Binary to denary conversion**'.

Converting denary to binary

To convert from denary to binary, follow these steps. Here is an example using the number 6.

- Write down the binary place values, and your target number in denary
  Target: 6

Place value	16	8	4	2	1
Number					

- Starting with the largest place value:
  - If the place value is less than or equal to the target, write a 1 and subtract the place value from the target to make a new target number, OR
  - If the place value is larger than the target, write a 0.
    Target: 6

Place value	16	8	4	2	1
Number					

- Move to the next value and repeat step 2 until either the target becomes 0, or there are no place values left
  Target: 6

Place value	16	8	4	2	1
Number	0	0			

Target: 6

New target: 6 – 4 = 2

Place value	16	8	4	2	1
Number	0	0	1		

Target: 2

New target: 2 – 2 = 0

Place value	16	8	4	2	1
Number	0	0	1	1	

Target: 0

Place value	16	8	4	2	1
Number	0	0	1	1	0

So the number 6 in denary is 00110 in binary. You could also write this as just 110, in the same way that the number 008 in denary could be written as just 8.

Workbook page 74: Complete Task B, '**Denary to binary conversion**'.

Tip

Another way to remember is to see each place as a binary switch and turn on (1) values you need, and off (0) those you don't. Adding these numbers together will create the denary total.

Overflow

Discuss 2

What happens if the number you want to store is too large for the number of bits you have available?

If you try to store the number 32, you will encounter a problem, because you cannot reach the target using the denary to binary conversion method.

Target: 32

New target: 32 – 16 = 16

Place value	16	8	4	2	1
Number	1				

Target: 16

New target: 16 – 8 = 8

Place value	16	8	4	2	1
Number	1	1			

Target: 8

New target: 8 – 4 = 4

Place value	16	8	4	2	1
Number	1	1	1		

Target: 4

New target: 4 – 2 = 2

Place value	16	8	4	2	1
Number	1	1	1	1	

Target: 2

New target: 2 – 1 = 1

Place value	16	8	4	2	1
Number	1	1	1	1	1

To solve this problem, you need to start with more place values! Each binary digit is called a **bit**, so to store the number 32 you will need six bits.

Place value	32	16	8	4	2	1
Number	1	0	0	0	0	0

Tip

The term 'bit' is actually short for **b**inary dig**it**! You may have heard it used before in phrases such as 64-bit computer system or 8-bit graphics.

You can work out how many different values it is possible to represent with a given number of bits in two ways. You can either add up all the place values and add 1, or you may find it faster to double the *largest* place value.

Discuss 3

Can you work out why you need to add up all the place values and then add 1 to find the number of different possibilities you can represent?

Tip

Computers use binary to store *all* data, from numbers and letters to images, documents and even programs.

Start your project

In the past, people would write letters to each other and send them using a postal service. Now it is more common to communicate via the Internet, using technology such as instant messages and emails. For your project in this chapter, you will create a booklet to explain the journey of a message, from when you type the letters on your computer or phone to when a 'virtual pen pal' on the other side of the world receives it.

Build 1:

In this lesson, you should aim to cover the first two bullet points in your booklet.

- Convert numbers between binary and denary.
- Explain why computers use binary to transmit data.

Later on in this chapter, you will find out how binary can be used to represent letters.

Workbook page 75: Complete the '**Reflection**' task.

Chapter 6.2 How are we connected?

What do we already know?

- Computers store all data as binary digits, or 'bits'
- Binary values are represented using electricity, either a high or a low voltage
- Fibre-optic cables allow signals to travel the world, even under the sea

Key terms

Fibre-optic cable – a type of cable that uses flexible glass fibres to transmit data as pulses of light

Copper cable – a type of cable that uses copper wire to transmit an electrical signal

Interference – disruption or alteration to an electrical signal

Transmit – send a signal from one place to another

WAN – Wide Area Network, a network that connects devices over a large geographical area, for example the internet

LAN – Local Area Network, connected devices in a small geographical area

PAN – Personal Area Network, a network that connects the devices within range of one person

Data cables

You have probably used a cable to connect to a network without even thinking about how it works. To **transmit** data across a long distance, you need a sturdy and durable cable. There are two main types of cable used for networks.

	Copper cables	Fibre-optic cables
Image		
Material	Copper	Glass fibres
Cost	Copper is cheap and easy to obtain.	Joining fibre optic cables together needs specialised equipment, and they are more expensive to install than copper cables.
How is data transmitted	Electrical currents	Pulses of light
Structure of the cable	A central copper wire, which is surrounded by insulation and a 'shield' made of woven metal, and a protective plastic coating to stop the metal getting wet.	A core of very thin but flexible glass fibres, protected by an outer ring of strengthening fibres to protect the core from damage. The inner core is surrounded by a light-absorbing cladding to prevent any light escaping or entering, which could cause problems with the signal.

	Copper cables	Fibre-optic cables
Typical use	Network cabling, e.g. in your school network or at home to connect to your router.	Cables travelling large distances, for example broadband cables entering your home from the street, or undersea cables between continents.
Information	The insulation helps to reduce electromagnetic **interference**, which is when the signal is disrupted or altered in some way. Interference is caused by a variety of things such as lightning, other signals or even solar flares. Copper cables can only be used across a certain distance before the electrical signal needs to be 'boosted'.	Fibre optic cables allow data to travel at the speed of light, and they are widely used for networking because they are flexible and can cover longer distances without losing signal quality.

Workbook page 76: Complete Task A, '**Copper and fibre optic cables**'.

Discuss 4

How can a cable connect you to someone on the other side of the world?

Differently sized networks

The internet is a Wide Area Network (or **WAN**), meaning it is a network that connects devices across a large geographical area – in the case of the internet, almost the entire world. However, when you communicate with someone in a different country, you don't rely on one single cable to connect you. Instead, the internet is made up of lots of different smaller networks, all joined together so that they can communicate.

Figure 6.2.3 A wide area network covers a large geographical area.

A Local Area Network (or **LAN**) is a network that connects devices in one physical location. Your school probably has a LAN that connects all of its devices, including desktop computers, laptops, tablets, and other hardware such as servers and printers.

Everyone in the school is given access to the LAN and this means that they can share the resources available: for example, you may save your work onto a school server. For security reasons, people outside the school community do not have access to the school's network. However, the school's LAN is connected to the internet (WAN), allowing users to communicate and access online resources.

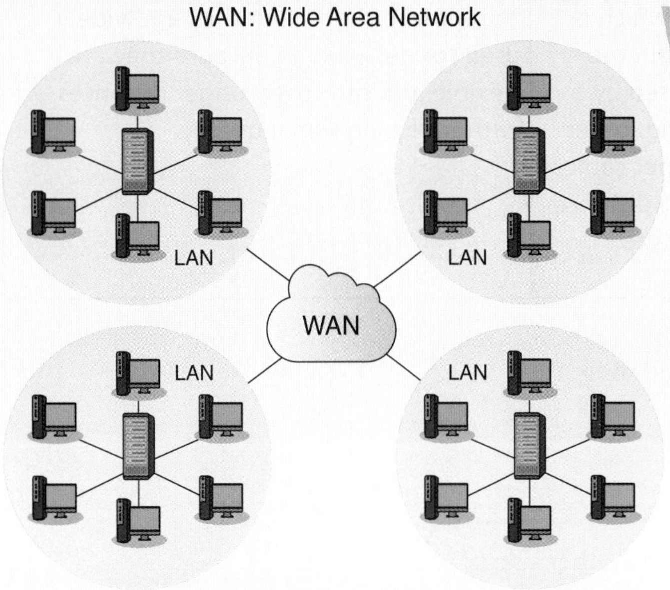

WAN: Wide Area Network

Figure 6.2.4 LAN networks connected as a WAN.

When you use personal devices such as your smartphone, this is called your Personal Area Network (or **PAN**). A PAN connects all of the devices in range of an individual. For example, someone who works in a home office may listen to music via wireless headphones and smartphone, work on their wireless laptop and track their daily exercise using a smartwatch. All of these connected devices become a personal area network.

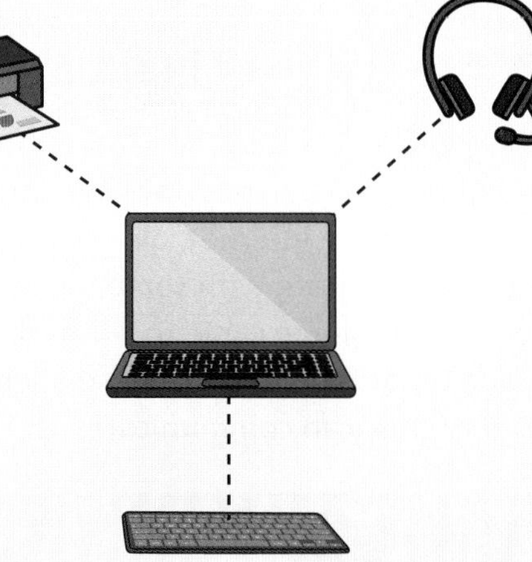

Figure 6.2.5 A personal area network.

Workbook page 76: Complete Task B, '**PAN, LAN or WAN?**'.

Build 2:

In your project booklet, cover the following objectives:

- Explain the differences between copper and fibre optic cables.
- Explain what interference is, and how it affects data being sent via a cable.
- Explain the difference between PAN, LAN and WAN.

You can draw a diagram or diagrams to help with your explanation.

Workbook page 77: Complete the '**Reflection**' task.

Chapter 6.3 ASCII

What do we already know?

- Computers communicate via cables, either as electrical signals or pulses of light
- The data transmitted across a network is in binary

Key terms

ASCII – American Standard Code for Information Interchange, a commonly used format for encoding characters on a computer

Unicode – a character encoding format that can encode characters in any language

Talking in numbers

Investigate 2

Can you communicate an English word to a partner, using only one hand? Your teacher will give you the instructions for this task.

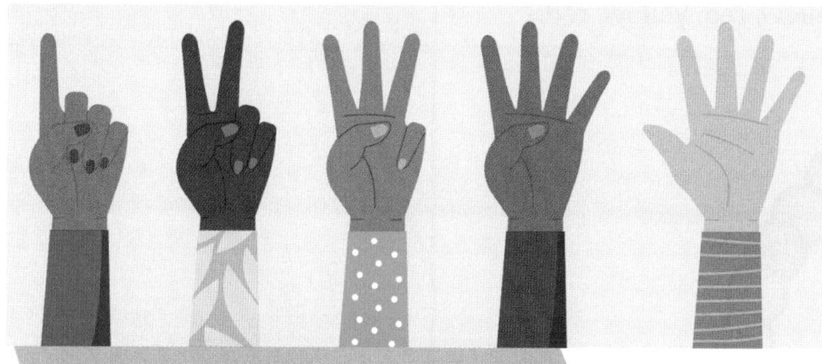

Figure 6.3.1 Communicating using only one hand.

Workbook page 78: Complete the '**Reflection**' task.

ASCII

When people began to communicate using computers, it was necessary to agree on a format to exchange information. Without a common format, computers might have different ways of representing letters, which could result in some very confusing communication!

In 1963, a format called ASCII was agreed in the USA. Each letter in the Latin alphabet (the letters A–Z) has a corresponding number code, and the number codes can be stored in binary. Capital letters A–Z have different number codes to lowercase letters. Your teacher will give you a worksheet with the ASCII codes for the letters in the alphabet.

Workbook page 79: Complete Task A, '**Write your name using ASCII**'.

Build 3:

Use the materials provided by your teacher to create a piece of jewellery representing your name in ASCII.

- Choose one colour to represent a 0, and a different colour to represent a 1.
- Begin with a single bead in a third different colour to represent the start of your message.
- Use your answer to Workbook page 79 Task A, where you wrote down the ASCII representation of each character in your name, in binary.
- For each character, add beads in the correct order to represent the ASCII code for that character.

You could use yellow to represent 0s and red to represent 1s. So, if your name begins with T, you could represent the uppercase letter T as yellow, red, yellow, red, yellow, red, yellow, yellow.

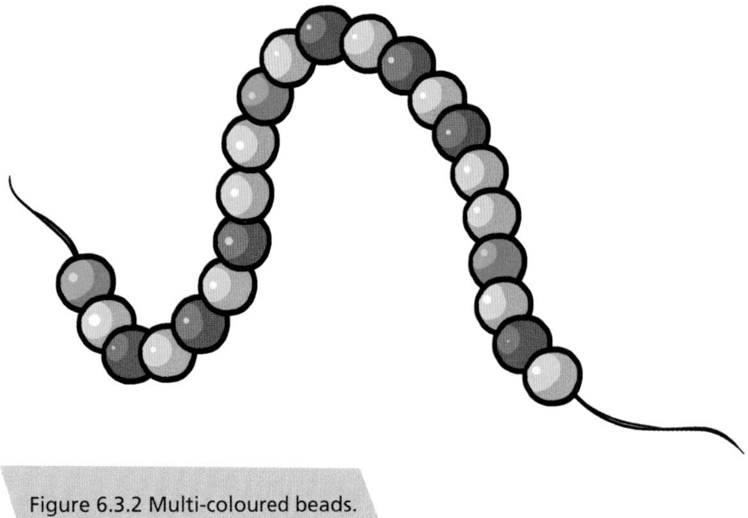

Figure 6.3.2 Multi-coloured beads.

Build 4:

In your project booklet, add information to meet the following objectives:

- Demonstrate how to write a word using ASCII.
- Convert ASCII codes back to letters and other characters.

What do we already know?

- When it is appropriate to use certain types of communication e.g. GIFs and emojis
- Text data is transmitted using an agreed format, e.g. ASCII

Key terms

Instant message – a short text-based message that is sent immediately, allowing them to be used for a real-time conversation

Live stream – to broadcast an online event as it happens; for example, someone playing a video game, or presenting to the camera

Social media – a website or an app that allows users to share text, image and video content with others they are connected to

Voice chat – a method of online communication via speech, often involving joining a channel with a specified theme

Online communication media

Discuss 5

If you want to communicate via the internet with someone in another country, what methods can you use?

Instant messaging apps are popular because they allow users to send short text-based messages, which are sent immediately via the internet. Examples of instant messaging services include WhatsApp, WeChat and Telegram. Some apps allow you to send encrypted messages or provide the ability to select GIFs or emojis as part of your message.

Social media platforms allow users to share text, images and video content with others who they are connected with. Examples include TikTok, Facebook, X, Instagram and Moj. Some focus on sharing images or short video clips, whereas others primarily allow users to write text-based posts, perhaps accompanied by an image or a video. Content posted on social media is usually shared with a wide audience.

Figure 6.4.1 An instant messaging app.

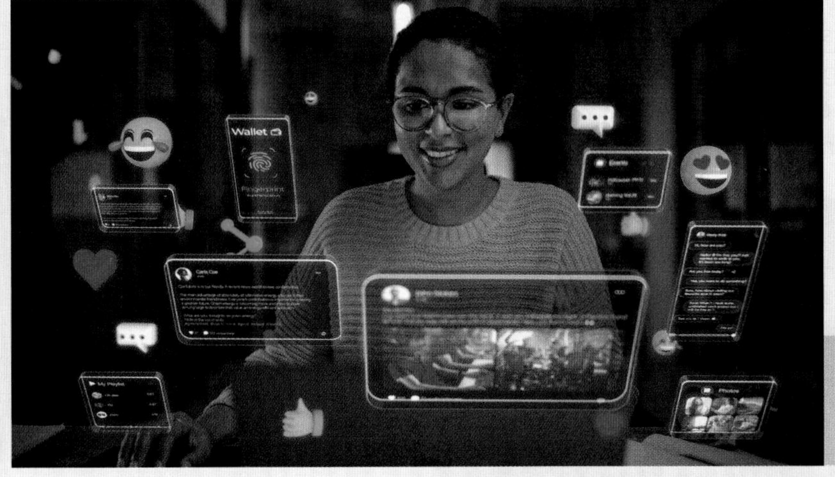

Figure 6.4.2 Social media platforms.

Stay safe

Before using a social media platform, check that you are over the age limit required. Many social media platforms require users to be over 13 years old to create an account.

A **video call** can be used to talk to someone who is not in the same location as you and is used widely for business meetings. Many people started to use these during the Covid-19 pandemic due to the restrictions in travel. It requires a device with a camera and a microphone and allows the participants to see and communicate with each other via a live video feed. Examples include Zoom, Google Meet and Facetime.

Figure 6.4.3 Six people taking a video call.

Voice chat servers, for example a Discord server, allow people to chat to other people with similar interests to them, or communicate verbally while they play video games. Some voice chat servers also provide the capability to chat in text, and provide moderation tools so that people can be removed or excluded from the server if they break the rules.

Figure 6.4.4 Voice chat equipment.

Lots of people of all ages play **online games**, either teaming up with or playing against people from other countries. Many games now offer built-in voice chat, and some also offer the ability to communicate in text-based messages. Some gamers choose to **live stream** their games, allowing other people to watch what they are doing as it happens, and comment on the gameplay.

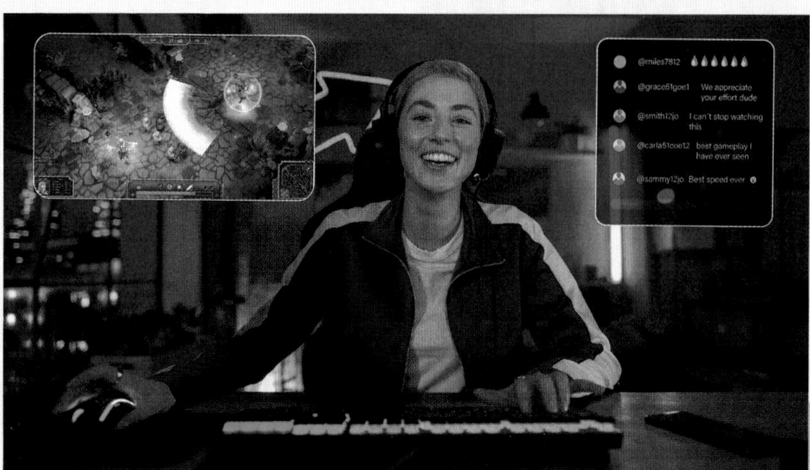

Figure 6.4.5 Live stream gaming.

Finally, **email** is a very common method of communication that is similar to a letter, except that the email arrives immediately after it has been sent. Documents and images can be attached to an email, and the same email can be sent to multiple people at once.

Figure 6.4.6 Email messaging.

Benefits and limitations

Investigate 3

Your teacher will divide you into groups and allocate your group one of the following contexts:

- School
- Friends your age
- Extended family

You will receive a piece of paper with a communication method at the top. Working together, write down as many benefits and limitations as you can think of for the context that you have been given. Add a key showing which context your pen colour represents.

Instant messaging ● = School

Benefits	Limitations
Teachers can be contacted quickly in an emergency	Cannot be used to send long documents Teachers should not share their phone number with pupils

Figure 6.4.7 Example work.

Workbook page 80: Complete Task A, '**Choose and justify a communication method**'.

Build 5:

In your project booklet, write about the method of communication you would use with your virtual pen pal. Make sure you cover the following objective:

- Describe the benefits and limitations of at least one method of online communication.

Workbook page 81: Complete the '**Reflection**' task.

Chapter 6.5 Data transmission

What do we already know?

- Computers store and transmit all data in binary
- Signals transmitted via copper cables can be affected by electrical interference
- Data to be transmitted is broken down into packets and the packets are reassembled at the destination
- A packet is a small amount of data transmitted over a network

Key terms

Compression – reducing the size of a file without affecting its contents

Echo check – a test to see whether data has been transmitted correctly, which repeats the data back to the sender and checks for differences

Packet – a chunk of data being transmitted across a network, e.g. the internet

Run length encoding (RLE) – a compression method that allows files with repeating patterns to potentially be stored more efficiently

Transmission error – a problem that occurs when data is sent across a network

Echo check

Data to be transmitted across a network is broken down into a series of numbered packets. Each of these is sent individually and then the **packets** are reassembled into the correct order at the destination. Packets of data are sometimes affected by interference during the journey; this is known as a **transmission error**. You may have seen this happen when videos you are streaming do not display correctly or experience a 'glitch'.

Figure 6.5.1 A video loading glitch.

One way for the computer receiving the data to check whether the data it has received is correct is by performing an **echo check**. This type of check repeats the data it has received back to the sender, and then the sender checks whether there were any differences. Video streaming uses the UDP protocol (mostly) rather than TCP/IP therefore there is no checking of data in the way suggested.

Role play 1

Work with a partner. Your teacher will give you a message to transmit to your partner. Perform an echo check to see whether the data has arrived correctly. Write your message down in your Workbook.

Workbook page 82: Complete Task A, '**What was the message?**'.

Compression

If less data is transmitted, there are fewer opportunities for transmission errors to occur. Some files can be **compressed** or reduced in size, with minimal effects on their contents. You will probably already be familiar with some types of compression. Here are some common examples:

.jpg	Image file
.zip	Archive file (contains more than one document)
.mp3	Audio file
.mp4	Video file

Run-length encoding

One compression method is called **run-length encoding**. It is most helpful for data where there are lots of repeating patterns. Consider an image similar to the one you used during the previous activity:

```
WWWWWWWWWWWWWWWRRRRRWRRRRRRRWYYYYYWGYYBYYGGYYBYYG
```

To encode the message, start with the first letter. Write down the letter, and then the number of times it occurs consecutively (one immediately after another). Repeat this until you have encoded the whole message.

For example, in this message, the first piece of data is W and it occurs 15 times consecutively, so instead of WWWWWWWWWWWWWWW you would write W15. Here is the full run-length encoded message:

```
W15R5W1R7W1Y5W1G1Y2B1Y2G2Y2B1Y2G1
```

Workbook page 82: Complete Task B, '**Run-length encoding**'.

Tip

If you are run-length encoding a message that spans more than one line, ignore the line break and continue as if the whole message were written on a single line.

Role play 2

Repeat the echo check exercise, but this time transmit the compressed message instead.

The message you have been transmitting is in fact a picture! Here is the image represented by the message above, with W as white, R as red, Y as yellow, G as grey and B as brown.

Workbook page 83: Complete Task C, '**Decode the message**'.

Workbook page 83: Complete the '**Reflection**' task.

Build 6:

In your project booklet, add information to meet the following objectives:

- Describe an echo check, and explain why it is used by a computer.
- Explain the word 'compression'.
- Use run-length encoding to compress some data.
- Uncompress some data that has been run-length encoded.

You could include a photograph of your run-length encoded picture if you wish.

Chapter 6.6 Finish your booklet

What do we already know?

- How to create a document to meet a brief

In this chapter, you have learned that you can send a message from a computer that can be read almost instantly by a virtual pen pal on the other side of the world. You have described each part of the message's journey – now it is time to bring all of that work together.

In this lesson, you will complete your booklet to explain the journey of a message.

Build 7:

Check the project brief from the start of this chapter. Have you covered all of the objectives? Are there any parts of your booklet that would benefit from some extra information or perhaps a diagram?

Figure 6.6.1 A student showcasing their work.

Showcase

Show your finished booklet to the group. Explain which part of the booklet you are most proud of, and why.

Workbook page 85: Complete Task A, '**Feedback**'.

Workbook page 86: Complete the '**Reflection**' task.

Well done! You have completed Chapter 6, 'Connect the world'.

In this chapter you:

- ☑ converted numbers between binary and denary
- ☑ learned about two types of network cable – copper and fibre optic
- ☑ found out that networks can be very large like a WAN, or focused around one person like a PAN
- ☑ wrote your name using ASCII and communicated a message using beads
- ☑ considered the different ways you can communicate online and their benefits and limitations
- ☑ role played an echo check to test whether data was transmitted correctly
- ☑ learned about compression, and how to compress using run-length encoding
- ☑ created a booklet to tell the story of how it is possible to send a message to a friend anywhere in the world.

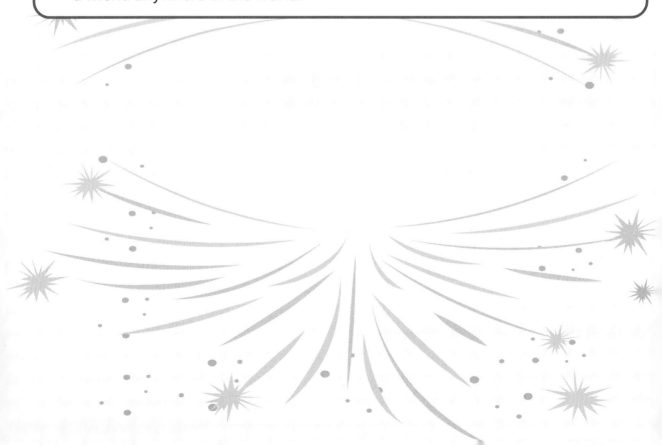

Congratulations!

Key terms

ASCII – American Standard Code for Information Interchange, a commonly used format for encoding characters on a computer

Binary – a number system that represents numbers using only two values: 0 and 1

Bit – a single **b**inary dig**it**, either 0 or 1

Compression – reducing the size of a file without affecting its contents

Copper cable – a type of cable that uses copper wire to transmit an electrical signal

Denary – the familiar base-10 number system, which uses the digits 0–9

Echo check – a test to see whether data has been transmitted correctly, which repeats the data back to the sender and checks for differences

Fibre optic cable – a type of cable that uses flexible glass fibres to transmit data as pulses of light

Instant message – a short text-based message that is delivered immediately, allowing them to be used for a real-time conversation

Interference – disruption or alteration to an electrical signal

LAN – Local Area Network, a network that connects devices in one physical location, for example a school or an office

Live stream – to broadcast an online event as it happens; for example, someone playing a video game, or presenting to the camera

Packet – a chunk of data being transmitted across a network, e.g. the internet

PAN – Personal Area Network, a network that connects the devices within range of one person

Place value – the value that a digit has because of its position ('place') in the number

Run length encoding (RLE) – a compression method that allows files with repeating patterns to potentially be stored more efficiently

Social media – a website or an app that allows users to share text, image and video content with others they are connected to

Transmission error – a problem that occurs when data is sent across a network

Transmit – send a signal from one place to another

Unicode – a character encoding format that can encode characters in any language

Voice chat – a method of online communication via speech, often involving joining a channel with a specified theme

WAN – Wide Area Network, a network that connects devices over a large geographical area, for example the internet

Reflect: What do you now know that you didn't know before?

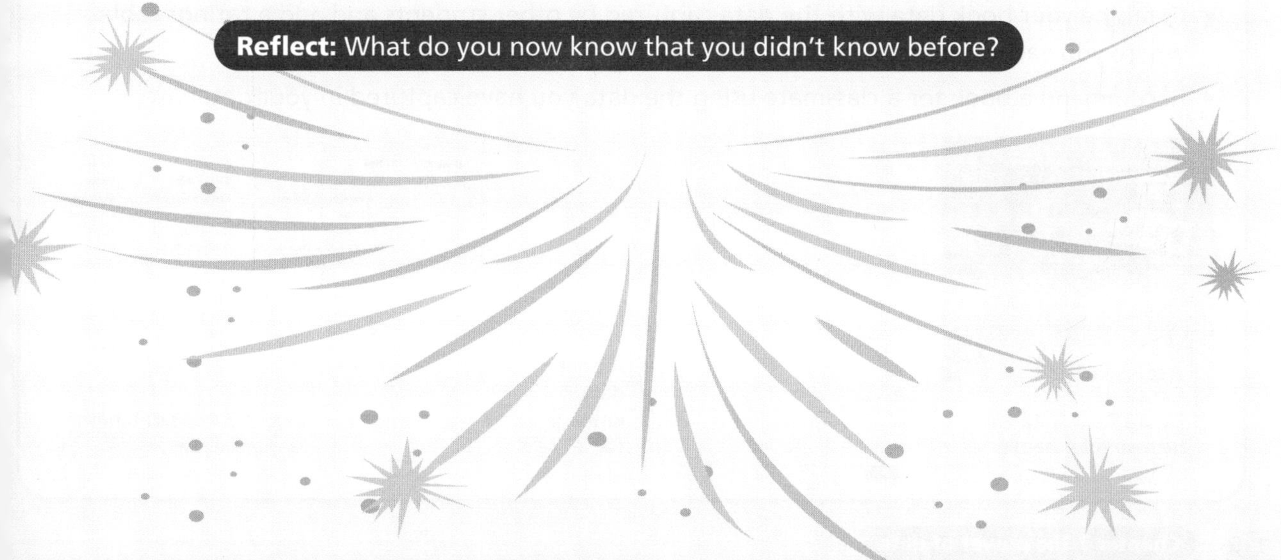

Chapter 7 The power of data

Project: Library database

In this chapter, you will:

- investigate a paper-based library cataloguing system and compare it with a modern library database system
- use a linear search algorithm to find data in a list, and explain when searching algorithms are needed
- design a data collection form to collect data about books
- learn about different methods of data validation
- create a digital form, including adding data validation
- work collaboratively with a group to generate some book ratings data
- use your book ratings data to generate a book recommendation
- define machine learning and learn how it is used to recommend things.

End of chapter project: Library database

In this chapter you will work together with a group to create a library database and input some data about books. You will then use the database to recommend a book to one of your classmates.

- Create a data capture form to gather the following information about each book: title, author, year of publication, genre
- Choose an appropriate form input for each piece of information
- Include at least one type check, length check and presence check on your data capture form
- Input data on ten books to create a single table database
- Combine your book data with the data captured by other students and add a ratings table where you each rate the books you have read
- Recommend a book for a classmate using the data you have captured in your database

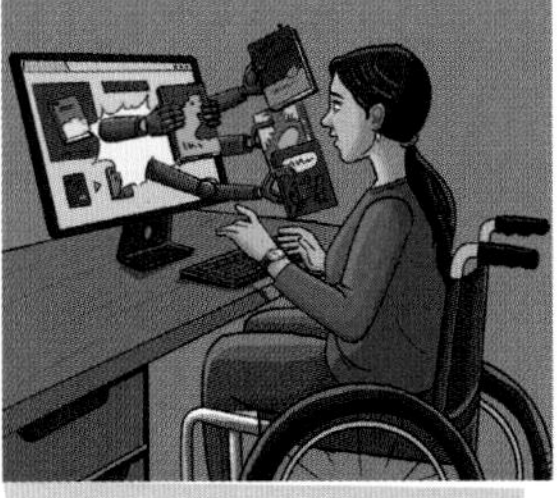

Figure 7.0.1 A student browsing for books.

Figure 7.0.2 A book data entry form.

	A	B	C	D
1	Book ID	Title	Author	Genre
2	1	The Hobbit	J R R Tolkien	Fantasy
3	2	The Wind in the Willows	Kenneth Grahame	Childrens
4	3	The Lorax	Dr Seuss	Childrens
5	4	Little Women	Louisa May Alcott	Family
6	5	Roll of Thunder, Hear My Cry	Mildred D. Taylor	Family
7	6	If You Come Softly	Jacqueline Woodson	Romance
8	7	Legend	Marie Lu	Adventure
9	8	The Fault in Our Stars	John Green	Romance
10	9	The Crossover	Kwame Alexander	Family
11	10	Six of Crows	Leigh Bardugo	Fantasy
12	11	The Lightning Thief	Rick Riordan	Fantasy
13	12	Firekeeper's Daughter	Angeline Boulley	Thriller
14				

Figure 7.0.3 A database of popular books.

Chapter 7.1 Keeping records

What do we already know?

- There are different data types, including integer, real, string and Boolean
- How to search for information using a search engine

Key terms

Database – an organised collection of data, usually stored on a computer

Record – a piece of information written down in a permanent form, to be used for later reference

Keeping records

Humans have been keeping **records** for thousands of years. The earliest records that have been found are stone tablets found in modern day Egypt and Iraq. The tablets recorded who owned various animals and crops, and date back more than 5,000 years.

Figure 7.1.1 Ancient Egyption tablet.

Many countries have census records of their population and where people lived, also dating back thousands of years. For example, in England a survey was recorded in 1086, called the Domesday Book, that lists the names of families living in each area across the country. It was used to calculate taxes owed to the King at that time.

Figure 7.1.2 The Domesday Book.

As paper became affordable and widely available and literacy improved, people began to use paper systems for keeping records. Libraries used cards to catalogue the books they owned so that people could find them.

Figure 7.1.3 An example of paper records.

Investigate 1

Using your research skills, find out how a library cataloguing system using paper cards works.

PUBLIC LIBRARY

TOLKIEN, J.R.R.

The Hobbit
London: George Allen and
Unwin 1937. 310 p

823.912

1. Fantasy - Fiction
2. Children's - Fiction

Figure 7.1.4 A library catalogue card.

Workbook page 89: Complete Task A, '**Label the catalogue card**'.

Workbook page 89: Complete the '**Reflection**' task.

A modern library

The area you live in probably has a library from which you can borrow books, or you may be lucky enough to have a library at your school. Nowadays, all the data about the books that a library has available is usually stored on a computer **database**. Finding a specific book is much quicker and easier than it would have been even as recently as 30 years ago.

Investigate 2

Find out how books are catalogued in a modern library. What are computers used for? Which tasks still need to be carried out by a human?

Workbook page 90: Complete Task B, '**Compare library systems**'.

Evaluate the two systems

Design 1

Create a poster for your classroom wall, explaining and evaluating the card and computerised library database systems. Include the benefits and any drawbacks.

Chapter 7.2 Linear search

What do we already know?

- The data stored about books in a library cataloguing system
- How to interpret an algorithm presented in pseudocode
- The value stored in a constant does not change while the program is running

Key terms

Dry run – simulate how an algorithm will run by tracing how the value of each variable changes

Linear search – an algorithm that checks each item in a list in turn until the search item is found, or the end of the list is reached

Searching algorithm – a method of finding a specific item in a list

Trace table – records how the values of variables in an algorithm change as the steps of the algorithm are followed

One of the main purposes of a library is to organise books so that relevant information can be found by the person who is searching for it. It would not be much use for a library to keep thousands of books but be unable to find any of them! To find a specific item in a list, you use a **searching algorithm**.

Linear search

A **linear search** is a searching algorithm that works through a list, inspecting each item in turn and comparing it with the item being searched for. The search ends either when the item is found, or the end of the list is reached.

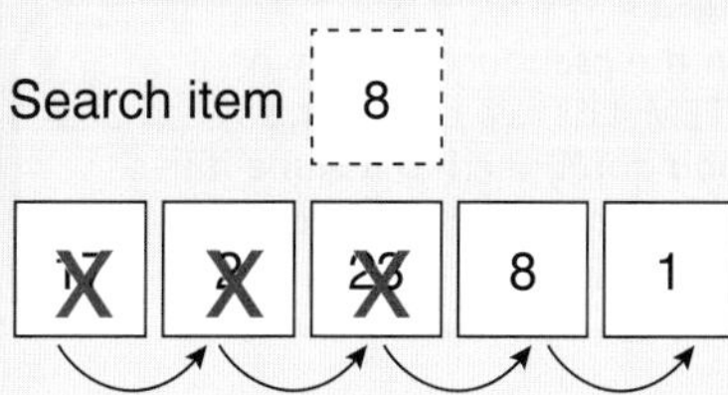

Figure 7.2.1 An example of a linear search.

In this example, the search item was compared to items in the list four times before it was found: 17, 2, 23 and 8. We can say that the number was found after four comparisons.

Tip

If the search item is compared to itself in the list, that still counts as a comparison.

Role play 1

Your teacher will choose some volunteers to role play a linear search as a demonstration for the class.

Workbook page 91: Complete Task A, '**Describe a linear search in words**'.

Trace a linear search

Nikesh has written some pseudocode for a linear search. He has added a line number at the start of each line.

```
01 ITEM_LIST = [17, 2, 23, 8, 1]
02 search_item = INPUT item you are searching for
03 FOR EACH item IN ITEM_LIST
04    IF item EQUALS search_item
05        OUTPUT "Found it"
06    ENDIF
07 NEXT item
```

Tip

Include line numbers in your pseudocode so that you can refer to a specific line of code in a trace table.

You can **dry run** an algorithm by recording how the values of the variables change as the steps of the algorithm are followed. You record the results in a **trace table**.

In a trace table, you need a column for the line number, the name of each variable, a condition result column and an output column.

Nikesh tested his algorithm by dry running the code and recording the results in a trace table.

Line	search_item	item	Condition	OUTPUT
01				
02	2			
03		17		
04			False	
06				
07		2		
03				
04			True	
05				Found it
06	...			

Tip

In the pseudocode shown, ITEM_LIST is a constant, so you don't need to include it in the trace table as its value will not change.

Tip

When you get used to drawing trace tables, if there is nothing to record on a particular row you can leave that row out.

Workbook page 91: Complete Task B, '**Answer the questions about the trace table**'.

Modify the code

Nikesh's pseudocode does not give any output if the item being searched for is not in the list. He thinks he could add a Boolean variable to keep track of whether the search item was found or not.

```
found = False
```

Build 1:

Work together with a partner. Modify Nikesh's pseudocode so that it outputs a message if the search item was not in the list. Each of you should record the new pseudocode in your Workbook.

Workbook page 92: Complete Task C, '**Record the new algorithm**'.

Workbook page 92: Complete the '**Reflection**' task.

Chapter 7.3 Data capture forms

What do we already know?

- A database is an organised collection of data, stored on a computer
- How to evaluate the effectiveness of data capture forms
- Data in a spreadsheet can have validation rules applied to it, e.g. "number is greater than"

Forms

Libraries receive new books regularly. When a new book arrives, it needs to be added to the database so that people can find it and borrow it. To ensure that the correct data in the right format is input by the user, a **form** is used to collect the data. The form inputs need to be carefully chosen depending on the data required.

The simplest form input is a **text box**, which prompts the user to type in some text.

Title

Figure 7.3.1 A text box to input a title.

If the data that should be entered is a single choice from a list of options, **radio buttons** are provided so that the user can select exactly one option.

Genre

- ○ Fantasy
- ○ Horror
- ○ Romance
- ○ Sci-fi

Figure 7.3.2 A radio button selection.

Key terms

Checkbox – a form input which allows one or more choices to be made from a list of options

Form – a method of collecting specific data, often to be added to a database

Length check – checks that the length of the data typed in is within a range

Presence check – checks whether a form field has been filled in

Radio button – a form input which allows a single choice to be made from a list of options

Text box – a form input which accepts string data

Type check – checks that the data entered has the correct data type

Validation – data typed into a form is checked to see whether it is a sensible value

Sometimes radio buttons are used to represent a scale; for example, where a user is asked to rate something.

Rating

	1	2	3	4	5	
Terrible	○	○	○	○	○	Excellent

Figure 7.3.3 Radio buttons on a scale.

If the question allows several choices to be selected in a list, **checkboxes** are used instead.

Contact methods

- ☐ Email
- ☐ Telephone
- ☐ SMS
- ☐ Mail

Figure 7.3.4 A checkbox selection.

A checkbox might also be used to represent a Boolean value; for example, if the user is asked to agree to something.

Apply to join the library

☐ I agree to follow the library rules

Figure 7.3.5 A Boolean checkbox.

Data validation

It is important that the library database is as accurate as possible. If there are mistakes in the Information, people might not be able to find the book they need. However, even very careful people sometimes make mistakes, so good programmers add **validation** to their forms to check that the data that has been entered is *sensible*.

Type of check	Pass	Fail
A **presence check** checks that the form input has actually been filled in and not left blank by mistake.	Author * Jane Austen	Author * Your answer This is a required question
A **length check** is typically used on a text box input, and counts the length of the text that was typed in. It checks that the number of characters typed is within a specified range.	Title * Pride and Prejudice	Title * a The title you have entered is too short
A **type check** checks the data type of the data that was entered; for example, is it a string, integer or date? This is useful to make sure that all the data entered is consistent; for example, if an input asked the user to type in their age and they typed twelve, a type check would prompt them to change their answer to 12 to be consistent with the other data in the database.	Publication year 1813	Publication year abc You need to enter a year, for example 2024

Workbook page 94: Complete Task A, '**Would it be accepted?**'.

Design a data capture form

The librarian needs a data capture form to collect the data about new books.

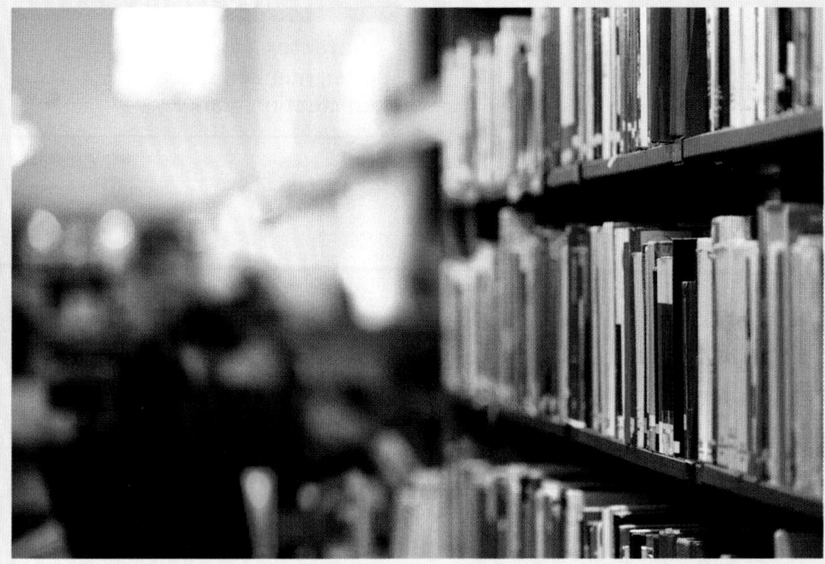

Workbook page 95: Complete Task B, '**Design a data capture form**'.

Showcase 1

Work with a partner for this task. Take it in turns to role play either a software developer presenting a form design, or a librarian giving feedback. The software developer should showcase their design to the librarian and explain why they chose each of the form inputs and validation methods. The librarian should use the information they learned in Lesson 1 about library databases to give feedback on the design.

Workbook page 96: Complete the '**Reflection**' task.

Chapter 7.4 Data validation

What do we already know?

- Data validation techniques including presence check, length check and type check

Key terms

Character – any single letter, number, space or punctuation mark

In this lesson, you will create your data capture form using software. Your teacher will tell you which software to use. This might be different from the software used in the examples.

Data validation

Re-create your design from Workbook page 95: Task B, 'Design a data capture form' as a digital form. You can add the validation you have planned directly into the form.

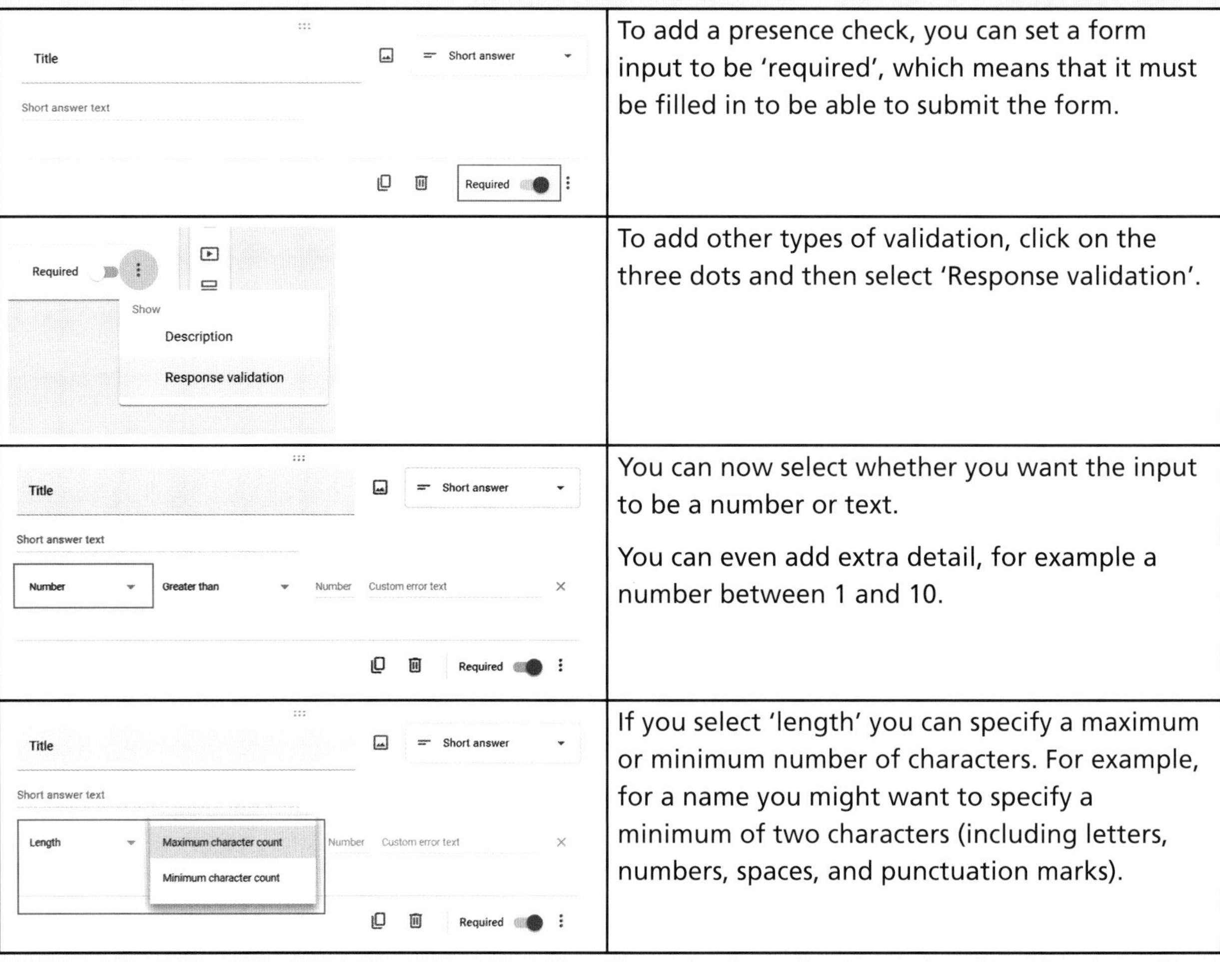

To add a presence check, you can set a form input to be 'required', which means that it must be filled in to be able to submit the form.

To add other types of validation, click on the three dots and then select 'Response validation'.

You can now select whether you want the input to be a number or text.

You can even add extra detail, for example a number between 1 and 10.

If you select 'length' you can specify a maximum or minimum number of characters. For example, for a name you might want to specify a minimum of two characters (including letters, numbers, spaces, and punctuation marks).

Build 2:

Your teacher will tell you which software to use to create a digital form using your design from the previous lesson. Make sure you add the validation that you planned in your design, and test that each validation check works correctly as you go.

Workbook page 97: Complete Task A, '**Draw and explain how you added data validation**'.

Collect data

Build 3:

Find and input data about ten different books, using the form you have built. You may need to research the details you need about each book online. Ask your teacher if you need help finding suitable websites. The data you type in will automatically be collected in a spreadsheet by the form software, with each form input in a separate column. Ask your teacher how to find the response spreadsheet in the software you are using if you are not sure, and check that all of the data has been captured correctly.

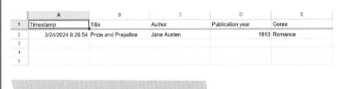

	A	B	C	D	E
1	Timestamp	Title	Author	Publication year	Genre
2	3/24/2024 9:26:54	Pride and Prejudice	Jane Austen	1813	Romance
3					
4					
5					

Figure 7.4.5 A book database entry.

Workbook page 98: Complete the '**Reflection**' task.

Chapter 7.5 Recommend a book

What do we already know?

- Design a single table database that include data attributes and data types
- Select an appropriate field to use as a primary key and describe its purpose

Key terms

Primary key – an assigned field in a database table that contains data that is both unique and not empty for every record

Table – a collection of related data, stored as columns and rows

Recommend a book

What data would you need to collect to be able to make a good book recommendation to someone who visits the library?

Discuss 1

Your teacher will allocate you a group. In your group, discuss what data you would need to collect to be able to recommend a book to someone.

Figure 7.5.1 A group discussion.

Workbook page 99: Complete Task A, '**Draw a mind map**'.

Gather some ratings

You have already gathered data on ten different books, and you can combine this data with the data collected by the other people in your group.

One way of recommending a book is to ask people to rate the books they have read, and then to use that data to recommend a different book.

Build 4:

Open the **table** containing data about books that you typed in the previous lesson. Save a separate copy of the table and add a new column called BookID at the start of the new table.

You are going to work together in a group to combine the data you have captured into a single table. Copy all of the book data collected by your group into a single file.

Then, give each book a unique number starting from 1 and note it down in the new BookID column. This is now the **primary key** of the book table, and it allows you to uniquely identify each book.

Tip

Some of the people in your group may have input data about the same book. Only include information about each book once in your new table – delete any duplicate data.

Tip

Some members of your group may have put their form input fields in a different order. Check when you combine the data that the data is in the correct columns.

Build 5:

Now create a *new* spreadsheet, and use it to create a table with the following headings:

BookID	Rated by	Rating (0–5)

Build 6:

Each member of the group will now rate the books they have read by typing a new row in the ratings table containing the ID number of the book, their name and their rating. If you have not read a particular book, do not add a rating. You will need to refer back to the books table to find the BookID for each book.

BookID	Rated by	Rating (0–5)
1	Iqra	5
1	Jagreet	2

In the next lesson you will use the rating data you have collected to recommend a book to someone in your class.

Workbook page 100: Complete the '**Reflection**' task.

Chapter 7.6 Machine learning

What do we already know?

- How to sort data in a spreadsheet
- How to search for data in a spreadsheet

Key terms

Big Data – an extremely large amount of data, which might be used to train a machine learning model

Machine learning – an area of computer science that uses algorithms and data to create software which can improve its own performance

Training – providing data to a machine learning algorithm so that it can recognise patterns in the data

Make a recommendation

Malik often visits the library to choose new books. The librarian would like to be able to give him recommendations for new books to read, based on his ratings of the previous books he has read.

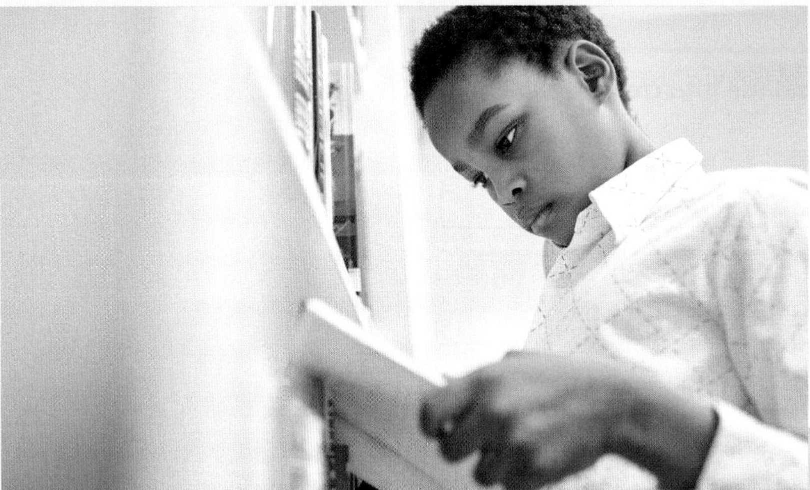

Figure 7.6.1 Malik.

Discuss 2

In your group, discuss how you could use the data you have gathered to recommend a book to Malik. Assume that you know Malik's ratings for the books he has already read.

Recommendation strategies

Investigate 3

Test each of the following strategies to recommend a book to person A.

1 Find A's highest rated book in the ratings table. Then, using the Book ID, look up the book's *genre* in the book table. The recommendation is another book in the same genre that A has not read.

2 Find A's highest rated book in the ratings table. Then, find another person (B) who also read that book. The recommendation is the book that B gave the highest score to.

3 Think of another strategy for recommending books and test it.

Tip

If anyone gave several books equally high scores, choose one at random.

Workbook page 101: Complete Task A, '**Make a recommendation**'.

Machine learning

In this lesson, you have seen how it is possible to make basic book recommendations using only a small amount of data in a database. **Machine learning** is an area of computer science that uses algorithms that are **trained** to spot patterns in huge amounts of data, and simulate the way that humans learn. The amount of data provided to machine learning models is so large that it is often referred to as **Big Data**.

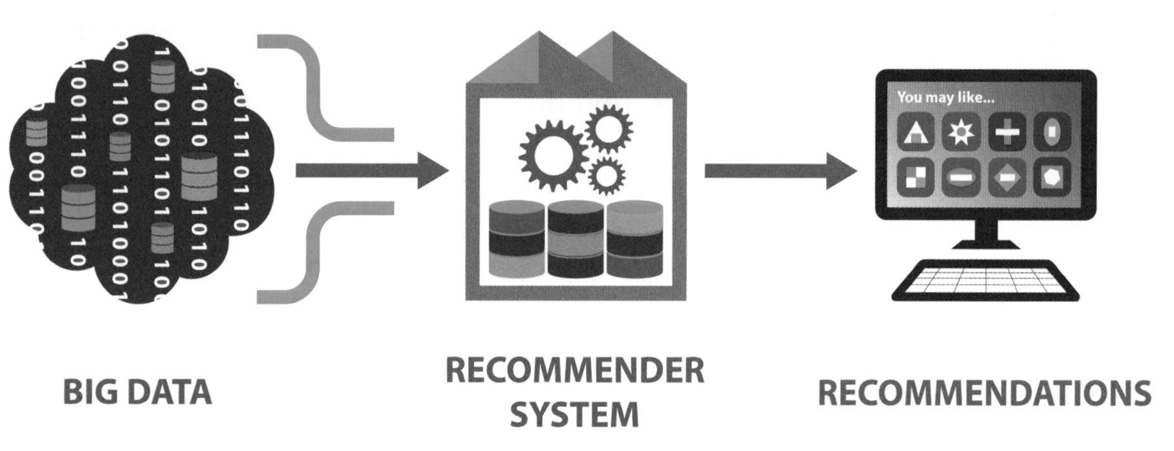

Figure 7.6.2 Analysing large amounts of data.

When you shop or watch a TV show, you are often asked to rate the thing you chose to buy or watch. Millions of people provide rating data, which is then fed into a machine learning model to make accurate predictions about other products and TV shows that you may like.

Workbook page 101: Complete Task B, '**Write a definition of machine learning**'.

Showcase 2

Share your book recommendation results with the class. How good do you think your recommendation strategy was?

Workbook page 102: Complete the '**Reflection**' task.

Well done! You have completed Chapter 7, 'The power of data'.

In this chapter you:

- ☑ found out how libraries used card catalogue systems and compared them to modern library databases
- ☑ used a linear search algorithm to find data in a list, and traced the pseudocode
- ☑ learned about the different types of form input and designed a form to collect data about library books
- ☑ learned about presence check, type check and length check validation
- ☑ created your data collection form and used it to input data about books
- ☑ worked collaboratively with a group to rate some books you have read
- ☑ used the book ratings data to generate a book recommendation for another member of the class
- ☑ found out how machine learning models can accurately recommend things you might like.

Key terms

Big Data – an extremely large amount of data, which might be used to train a machine learning model

Character – any single letter, number, space or punctuation mark

Checkbox – a form input that allows one or more choices to be made from a list of options

Database – an organised collection of data, usually stored on a computer

Dry run – simulate how an algorithm will run by tracing how the value of each variable changes

Form – a method of collecting specific data, often to be added to a database

Length check – checks that the length of the data typed in is within a range

Linear search – an algorithm that checks each item in a list in turn until the search item is found, or the end of the list is reached

Machine learning – an area of computer science that uses algorithms and data to create software that can improve its own performance

Presence check – checks whether a form field has been filled in

Primary key – an assigned field in a database table that contains data that is both unique and not empty for every record

Radio button – a form input that allows a single choice to be made from a list of options

Record – a piece of information written down in a permanent form, to be used for later reference

Searching algorithm – a method of finding a specific item in a list

Table – a collection of related data, stored as columns and rows

Text box – a form input that accepts string data

Trace table – records how the values of variables in an algorithm change as the steps of the algorithm are followed

Training – providing data to a machine learning algorithm so that it can recognise patterns in the data

Type check – checks that the data entered has the correct data type

Validation – data typed into a form is checked to see whether it is a sensible value

Reflect: What can you do now that you couldn't do before?

Chapter 8 Create with code 3

Project: Technology at work

In this chapter, you will:

- investigate the use of digital technology in a variety of workplaces
- understand what is meant by autonomous programming
- learn about radio communication
- use radio communication to send messages between two BBC micro:bits
- design a device that uses radio communication to be used in a workplace
- plan an algorithm with pseudocode
- learn how to dry run an algorithm
- devise a test plan with test data
- use the test plan to test whether your device works
- showcase your idea to another team.

End of chapter project: Technology at work

You are going to design a system to be used in a workplace. Your system should meet the following brief:

- The system should use two micro:bits.
- The micro:bits must communicate with each other via a radio signal.
- You can also use any of the other features of the micro:bit, for example the buttons or the LED matrix.

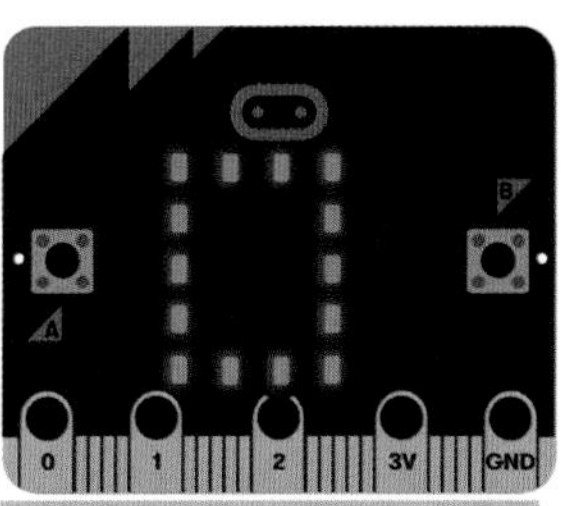

Figure 8.0.1 A micro:bit.

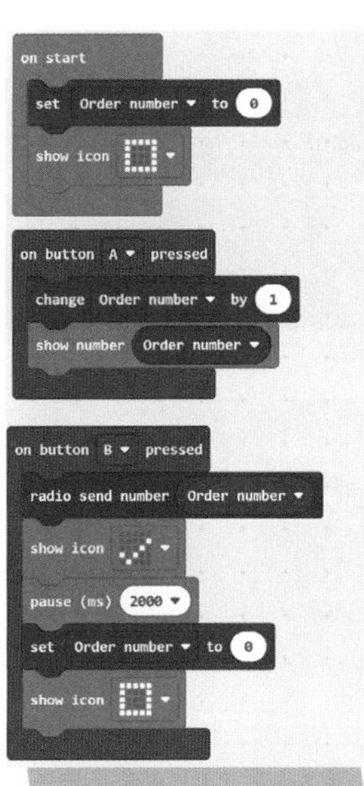

Figure 8.0.2 Examples of micro:bit button programming.

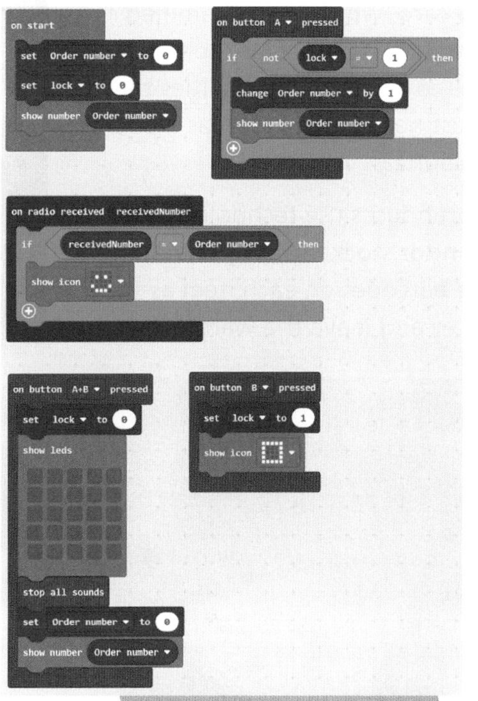

Figure 8.0.3 Examples of micro:bit radio programming.

Chapter 8.1 Digital technology in the workplace

What do we already know?

- Computer systems allow data to be input, processed, stored and output
- Hardware devices such as keyboards and monitors are used to input and output data

Key terms

Barcode – a series of stripes that contain data and can be scanned by a barcode reader device

Digital technology – any device or system that creates, stores or uses data

Radio Frequency Identification (RFID) tag – contains data that can be read via a radio signal when the tag is close to a reader

Digital technology in the workplace

Digital technology is any device or system that creates, stores or uses data. Some form of digital technology is now used in almost every workplace.

Discuss 1

What workplaces can you think of where digital technology is used?

Here are a few examples of how digital technology is used in different workplaces.

Many hotels now use electronic locks on the doors to their guest rooms. Guests can be given a key card, which is programmed to unlock a particular room as well as access other facilities the guest has paid for, such as a pool or sauna.

Warehouses use technology to monitor stock levels by scanning the barcodes on each item as they enter and leave the warehouse.

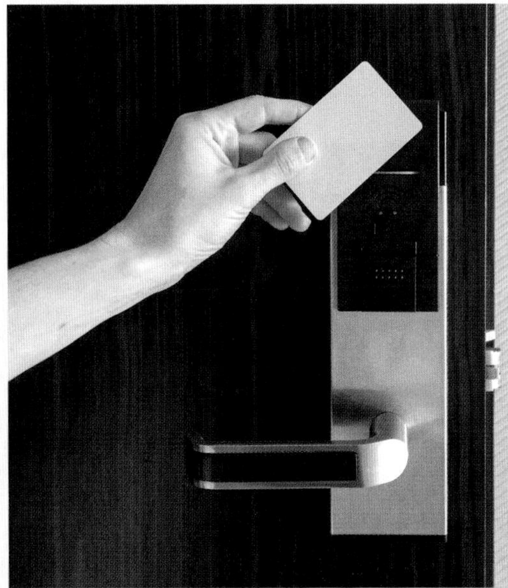

Figure 8.1.1 A hotel key card.

Figure 8.1.2 A warehouse barcode scanner.

Office workers can now use video conferencing software to collaborate with co-workers anywhere in the world. People can be seen and chat almost as if they were in the same room.

Figure 8.1.3 A video conference.

Some factories now use machines to perform parts of their production process. Robots are used for precise tasks, such as soldering a circuit board, and can be programmed to make different items.

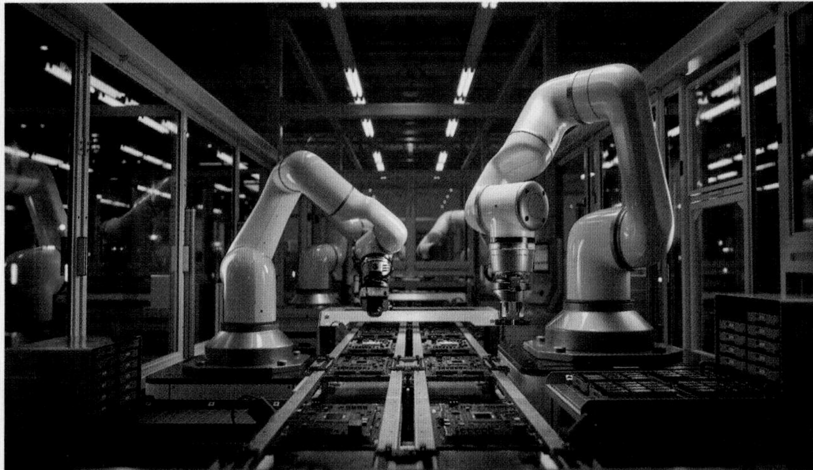

Figure 8.1.4 Example of robot manufacturing.

Shops allow customers to scan their own items using a handheld scanner, and then pay for them at an automated till. It is possible to enter a shop and purchase what you want without ever having to interact with a human.

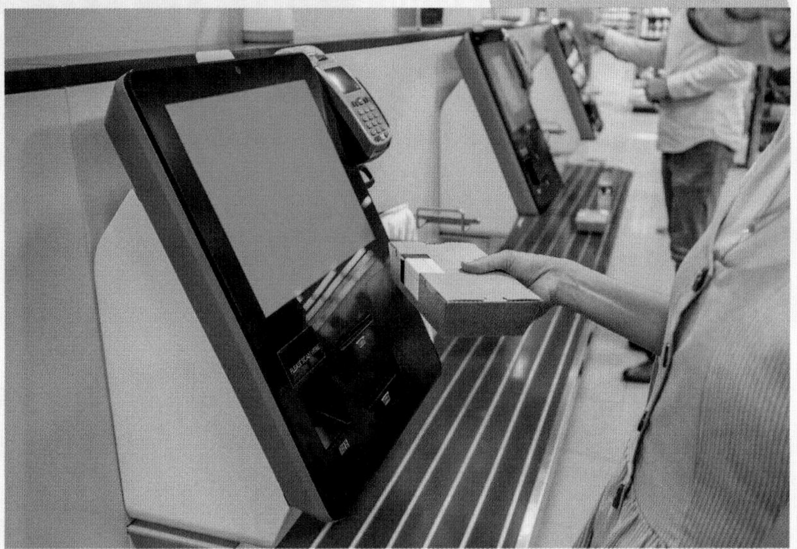

Figure 8.1.5 A supermarket self scanner.

Workbook page 104: Complete Task A, '**Mind map**'.

Hardware devices

Remember that digital technology uses data, so there needs to be a way for a human to input or output the data using a hardware device. Some workplace devices such as webcams and monitors are familiar, but some are highly specialised for the task they are used for. Here are some examples of more specialised devices:

Barcode scanners can be used to input data about a parcel or an item in a warehouse. Each item has an individual barcode, which, when scanned, associates it with data in a database such as how many of the items are available or which country the parcel has been sent to.

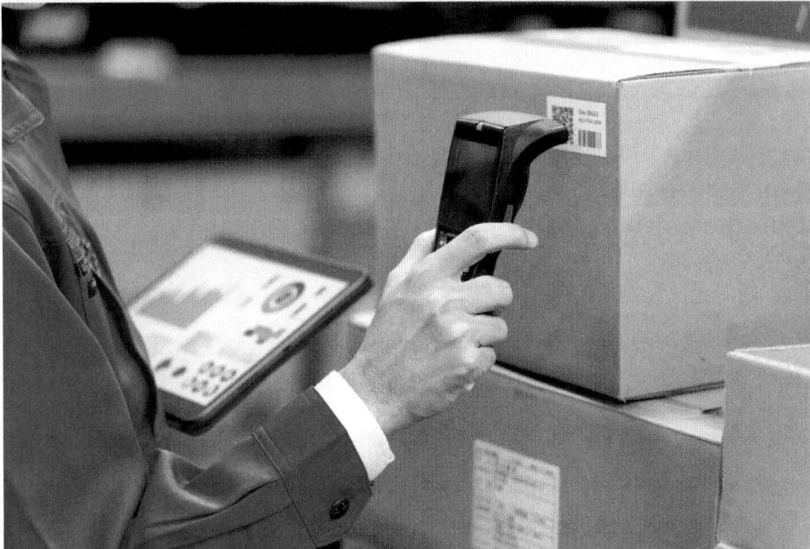

Figure 8.1.6 Scanning an item in a warehouse.

A **Radio Frequency Identification (RFID)** tag contains data that can be read by a RFID reader. The tags can be stuck onto items and action taken when they are close to a reader. You may have seen these kinds of tags stuck to expensive items in shops, which trigger an alarm when they pass through a sensor near the exit door.

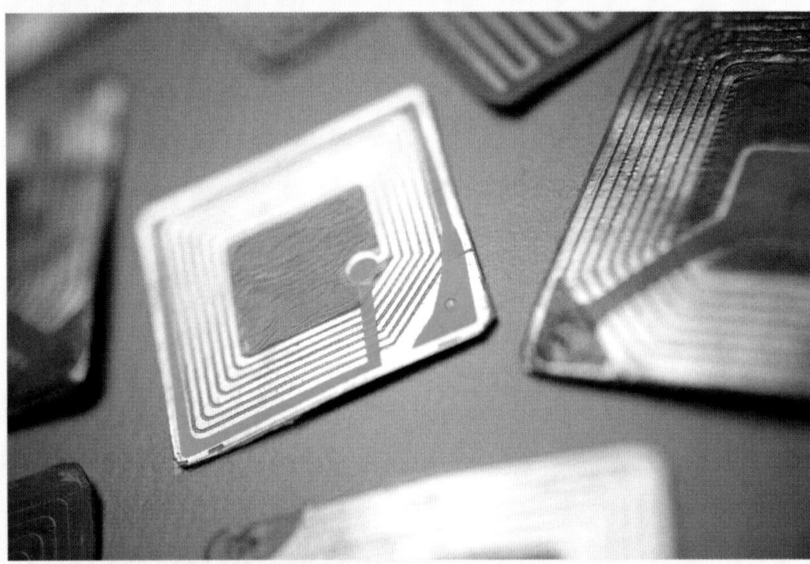

Figure 8.1.7 An RFID tag in clothing.

A label printer can be used to label items with barcodes, or to generate mailing addresses for customer orders. It can automatically print the label with the correct data for the next order, speeding up the process for the human selecting the goods. Label printers can also be used to quickly generate ID badges for visitors.

The robotic arms used in factories are sometimes either controlled or programmed by a human. A control panel is required to allow the human to input the instructions for the robot to carry out.

Figure 8.1.8 A barcode or QR code label printer.

Figure 8.1.9 An operator programming a robot.

Workbook page 105: Complete Task B, '**Hardware devices in the workplace**'.

Build 1:

Join together with the other students who have been focusing on the same workplace, to form a group. Using presentation software, create a presentation about the types of digital technology that are used in that workplace.

Workbook page 105: Complete the '**Reflection**' task.

Chapter 8.2 Autonomous programming and AI

What do we already know?

- AI can use existing data to produce outputs based on models
- Robots can work on tasks without the need for human input

Key terms

Artificial intelligence (AI) – the simulation of human intelligence by a machine

Automatic – the ability of a machine to perform a task without input from a human

Autonomous – the ability of a computer to perform a task without input from a human, but including the ability to react to circumstances as it finds them

Autonomous programming

In the previous lesson you learned that some workplaces use robots to perform tasks that would either be too difficult or too time-consuming for a human. Sometimes, these robots are controlled by humans, but robots can be programmed to act **autonomously** – this means they can perform some tasks without the need for human input.

Figure 8.2.1 An autonomous waiter.

Some restaurants use autonomous robots to serve food and drinks. Human input is needed to prepare and load the food and to tell the robot which table to take it to, and then the robot acts autonomously to deliver the food. The robot can calculate the path to the correct table and uses its sensors to collect information and react to the circumstances; for example, it will stop if a person walks in front of it, or an obstacle blocks its path.

Autonomous robots may use **artificial intelligence (AI)** to help them to make decisions required to perform tasks. Machine learning is a type of artificial intelligence that enables a computer to improve its own performance on a task **automatically**.

Automatic vs autonomous

Consider a food production line that uses a machine programmed to fill jars with tomato sauce. The machine is certainly programmed to work automatically – it can perform its task without human intervention. However, it is not *autonomous* like the restaurant robot. Imagine that one of the jars is missing or broken. The machine cannot detect or react to this change, and will squirt tomato sauce into the place where the jar should be.

Figure 8.2.2 A tomato sauce production line.

Workbook page 107: Complete Task A, '**Is it autonomous?**'.

Workbook page 107: Complete the '**Reflection**' task.

Think back to the presentation about uses of technology in a workplace that you created during the previous lesson.

- Are any of the uses of technology you covered *automated*?
- Can you think of any additional ways in which automation is used in this workplace?

Build 2:

Rejoin your group from the previous lesson. For each of the slides in your presentation, add an additional slide to explain whether or not the technology described uses automation.

Showcase 1

Showcase your presentation to the class. Each person in the group should take a turn to explain their slide, and then the rest of the class should decide whether the technology described uses automation.

Workbook page 108: Complete Task B, '**Automated or not?**'.

Chapter 8.3 Radio signals

What do we already know?

- Bluetooth is a protocol for communicating between devices over a short range

Key terms

Radio signal – a signal within a specific frequency band, used to transmit data

What is a micro:bit?

A micro:bit is a small device that can be connected to a computer and programmed to carry out a range of tasks. Different versions have different features, but all micro:bits have two buttons and a matrix of 25 LEDs.

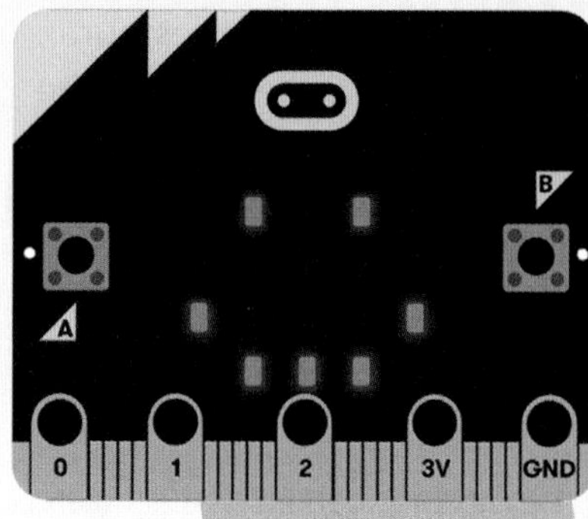

Figure 8.3.1 micro:bit LED smiley.

You may have used micro:bit devices before. In this chapter, you will program a micro:bit using Microsoft MakeCode editor, which looks like this:

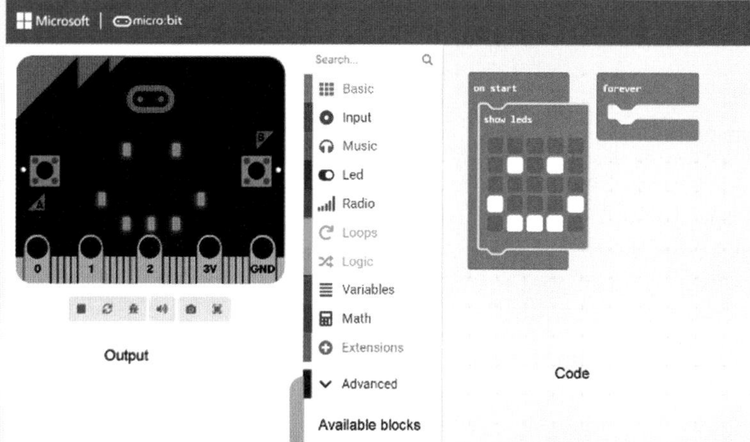

Figure 8.3.2 micro:bit LED programming block.

The interface is similar to Scratch. On the left is a micro:bit simulator, which you can use to run and test your programs, including things like pressing buttons. In the middle, you can see a list of the available block types and, if you click on each type, the available blocks. To write your code, you drag the blocks you want into the code area on the right.

What is a radio signal?

In a previous lesson you learned about Radio Frequency ID (RFID) tags, which can be attached to items. The data on the tag can be scanned as it passes a RFID reader.

If you have more than one micro:bit device, they can be programmed to communicate using **radio signals,** just like an RFID tag and RFID reader.

Your teacher will show you a demonstration of how this works.

Figure 8.3.3 micro:bits communicating via radio signals.

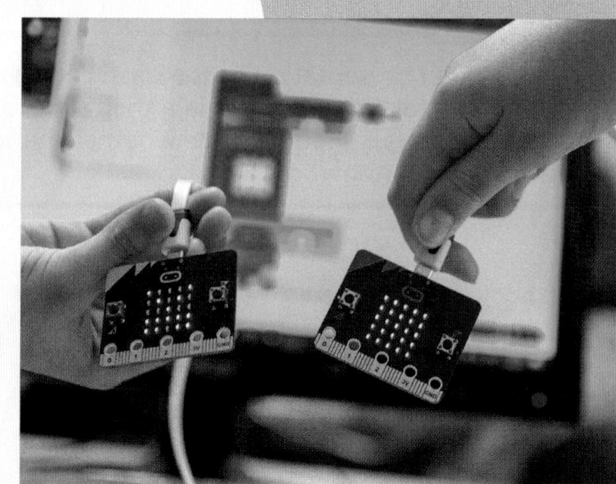

Send a radio signal

Open up the MakeCode editor for micro:bit – your teacher will tell you where this is. You will see that two code blocks have been added for you: `on start` and `forever`.

Click on the 'Radio' option in the menu to see the radio signal blocks you can use.

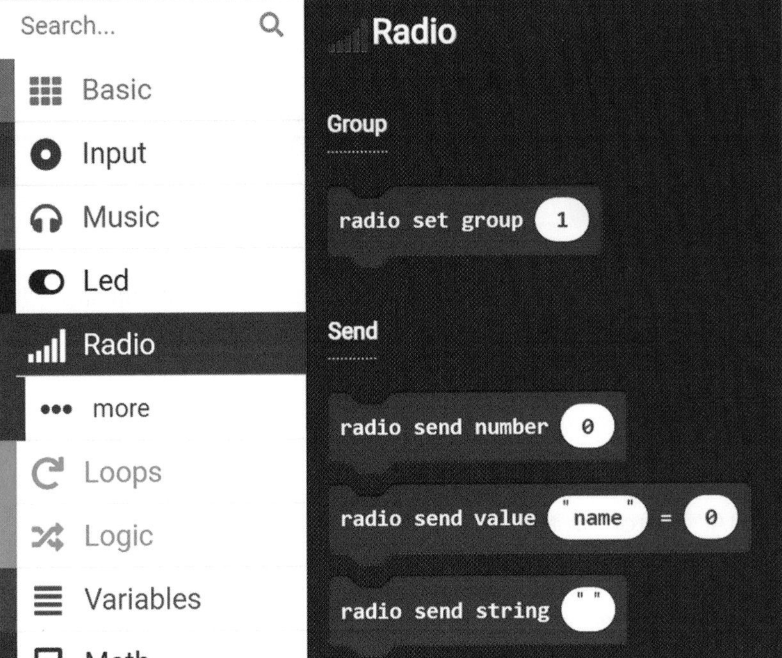

Figure 8.3.4 micro:bit radio blocks.

Build 3:

In pairs, write a program to send data between two micro:bits via radio signal.

- Drag the `radio set group (1)` block inside the `on start` block you already have. This tells the micro:bit to listen for messages on channel 1.
- Add an input block and a radio block, so that when button A on the micro:bit is pressed, the letter "A" is sent as a radio signal.

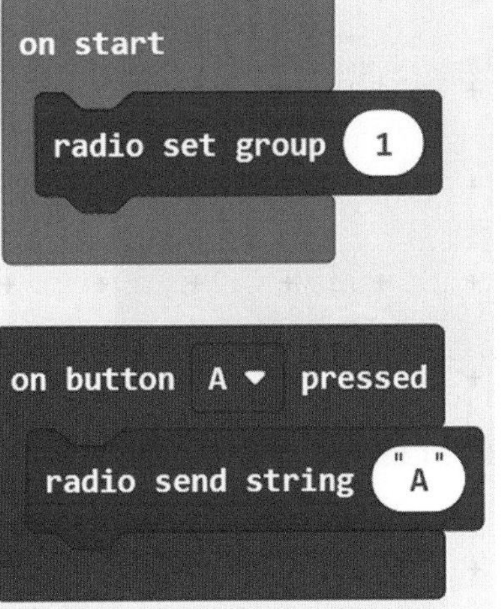

Figure 8.3.4 micro:bit radio and button blocks.

Tip

Your teacher may give you a different channel number to use, so that you don't receive messages from everyone in the class!

If you press button A on the on-screen micro:bit at this point, you will see a second micro:bit appear below, and an animation showing that you have pressed the button. However, nothing else will happen, because you need to add code to tell the micro:bit what to do when it *receives* the signal.

- Add some more code to tell the micro:bit to display the message it received on the LED matrix when it receives the signal.

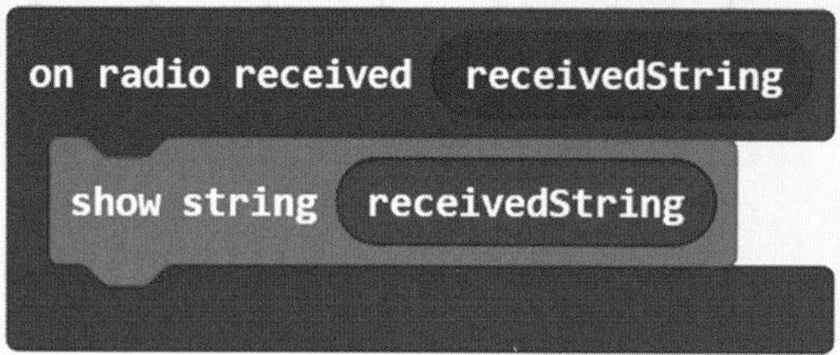

Figure 8.3.5 micro:bit radio receiving block.

- Test your program by clicking the "A" button on the micro:bit emulator. You should see the letter A appear on the second micro:bit below.

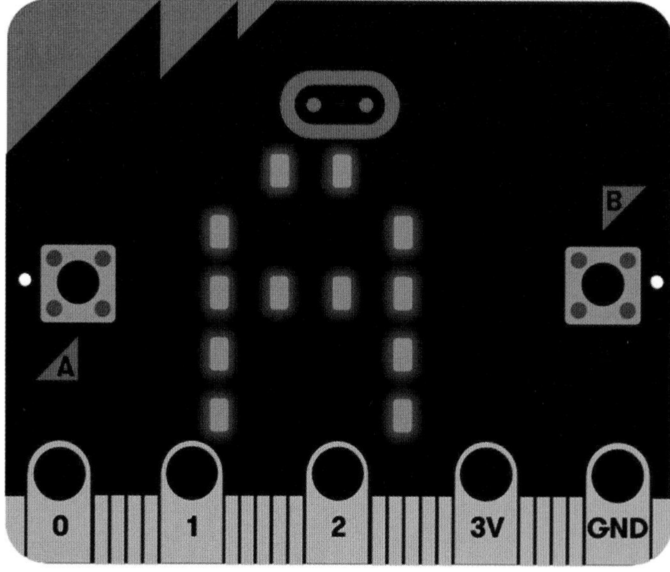

Figure 8.3.6 micro:bit LED A.

- Add some more code to your program so that the letter "B" is transmitted when the B button is pressed.
- Modify your program so that it sends a message instead of just a letter.

Tip

You can drag the `receivedString` variable out of its original position to make a copy of it.

Project brief

You are going to design a system to be used in a workplace. Your system should meet the following brief:

- The system should use two micro:bits.
- The micro:bits must communicate with each other via a radio signal.
- You can also use any of the other features of the micro:bit, for example the buttons or the LED matrix.

Discuss 2

Discuss with your partner how you could use the radio signal blocks on the micro:bit to design a device to be used in the workplace.

Workbook page 110: Complete Task A, '**Note down your ideas**'.

Working with your partner, choose one of the ideas you came up with. In your workbook, draw and explain the system. You will plan the code for the system during the next lesson.

Workbook page 110: Complete Task B, '**Design a system for use in the workplace**'.

Here is an example design for a system:

Our system will be used in ... a restaurant ... .

Describe briefly what the system does:

A customer will be given a micro:bit when they order, programmed with their order number. When their order is ready to collect, the chef will send a message and the customer's micro:bit will display a smiley face.

Write down a series of steps to describe how the system will work.

1. Select customer order number on the customer micro:bit
2. Select the order number that is ready on the chef's micro:bit
3. When order number is selected, chef's micro:bit transmits that number via radio
4. When the customer micro:bit receives a radio message containing its own order number, it displays a smiley face

Workbook page 111: Complete the '**Reflection**' task'.

Chapter 8.4 Design a workplace system

What do we already know?

- How to develop a program for a physical computing device
- You can use pseudocode to plan a program by using statements that have a clear and precise meaning, but are not written in any particular programming language
- You can simulate how an algorithm will run by tracing how the value of each variable changes – this is called a dry run

Key terms

Event-driven programming – a style of programming where all code is written to respond to events, for example when a button is pressed

Trigger – cause to happen

Divide up the tasks

In the previous lesson you wrote a description and a series of steps for your workplace system in your Workbook.

Workbook page 110: Task B, '**Design a system for use in the workplace**'.

You are going to continue working on your design during this lesson.

Workbook page 112: Complete Task A, '**Divide up the tasks**'.

Here is an example of the tasks that each Micro:bit needs to perform.

micro:bit 1 – Customer	micro:bit 2 – Chef
• Allocate order number • When I receive a radio message containing my order number, display a smiley face	• Select number of order that is ready to be collected • Transmit selected order number as a radio message

Plan in pseudocode

You and your partner should each take charge of the tasks for *one* of the micro:bits.

Unlike programs that you typically write in Python, the micro:bit is programmed to wait for and respond to events, such as buttons being pressed. This is called **event-driven programming**. Think about *when* the task you are writing pseudocode for needs to happen; for example, when a button is pressed, when a radio signal is received or when the program starts. You may need to write several separate blocks of pseudocode. You should use a heading to describe when each block of code is **triggered**.

Here is part of the pseudocode for the customer micro:bit used in the previous lesson.

```
1 WHEN the program starts:
2 SET order_number TO 0
3 SHOW order_number
4
5 WHEN button A IS PRESSED:
6 ADD 1 TO order_number
7 SHOW order_number
```

Tip

Adding a line number to each line of your pseudocode will help you when you dry run the code later.

Workbook page 112: Complete Task B, '**Write the pseudocode**'.

Dry running an algorithm

You can **dry run** an algorithm to check whether it does what you expect. You have done this before, in Chapter 7.

For example:

What I am testing: Input order number 1

Test input: Press A

Lines 1-3 always happen first as they are the code for "when the program starts"

Line	order_number	Input	Output
1			
2	0		
3			0
		A	
5			
6	1		
7			1

Then, the program waits for an input

The input received was A, so the block of code for "when button A is pressed" on lines 5-7 executes

Figure 8.4.1 Algorithm dry run trace table.

Workbook page 113: Complete Task C, '**Dry run your pseudocode**'.

Workbook page 113: Complete the '**Reflection**' task.

Tip

Make sure you always include any code labelled as "WHEN the program starts" first in your trace table – these are the lines highlighted in the table.

Build 4:

Using the pseudocode plan you have created and tested, start to write your code using the MakeCode editor.

Chapter 8.5 Test plans and test data

What do we already know?

- How to write and apply test plans; for example, by having columns to explain the test, the specific input and a specific expected output

Key terms

Valid data – data that should be accepted by a program

Invalid data – data that should *not* be accepted by a program

Test data

When you have built your program, you will need to test that it works correctly alongside your partner's program. **Valid data** is data that should be able to be input into a program if the program works correctly. However, when software engineers test software, they do not only test valid data – they also test **invalid data**, which is data that should *not* be accepted by a program.

Think back to the order system example from the previous lessons. The restaurant may only allow a maximum of nine different orders at any point in time, to avoid there being too much work for the chef. The customer's micro:bit could be tested to see whether it accepts both valid and invalid order numbers:

- **Valid data:** 5, 8
- **Invalid data:** 32, 66

Discuss 3

Why do you think it is helpful to test invalid data as well as valid data?

Build 5:

With your partner, continue to build your program according to your pseudocode design.

Test plan

When you have completed your program, work together with your partner to create a test plan for your system. Here is an example of a test:

#	Description	Input	Expected output	Result
1	On customer micro:bit, select a valid order number	Press button A 5 times	Numbers 1, 2, 3, 4, 5 displayed, changing each time the button is pressed	

Take care to use specific language when you describe each test. It should be possible for you to give your test plan to someone else who is not familiar with your system, and they should be able to understand what they are supposed to do, and what results to expect.

Workbook page 115: Complete Task A, '**Create a test plan**'.

Workbook page 116: Complete the '**Reflection**' task.

Chapter 8.6 Test your program

What do we already know?

- How to identify and debug errors in text-based programs; for example, spelling mistakes or missing characters
- How to test programs using a range of criteria

Key terms

Pass – the expected outcome of the test happens when the test is performed

Fail – the expected outcome of the test does not happen

Perform the tests

Investigate 1

Use the test plan you created in the previous lesson to test your program and record the results on Workbook page 115. For each test, make sure you note down whether the test **passes** or **fails** – in other words, is the expected outcome you noted down in the test plan what you actually see?

Workbook page 118: Complete the '**Reflection**' task.

Build 6:

Act on the results of your testing. Did any of your tests fail? Is there anything in your program that needs to be improved before you show it to another group?

Demonstrate your program

Figure 8.4.2 A wireless system to call customers when their food order is ready.

Showcase 2

Demonstrate your program to another group. Make sure you explain clearly:

- which workplace your system would be used in
- how the system works – if each micro:bit does something different, make sure to explain both.

While you are watching the other group's demonstration, answer the questions in the Workbook.

Workbook page 118: Complete Task A, '**Watch the demonstration**'.

Give the other team some feedback about their system.
For example:

- Do you think the system works properly, or are there any issues?
- Do you think the system would be helpful in the workplace?

Congratulations!

Well done! You have completed Chapter 8, 'Create with code 3'.

In this chapter you:

- ☑ investigated the use of digital technology in the workplace
- ☑ found out about radio frequencies and RFID tags
- ☑ thought about what makes a system autonomous
- ☑ designed a system to be used in a workplace
- ☑ wrote a piece of software using two interacting micro:bits
- ☑ wrote pseudocode to plan a program
- ☑ tested your pseudocode with a dry run
- ☑ wrote a test plan, including tests for invalid data
- ☑ tested your program and acted upon any tests that did not pass.

Key terms

Artificial intelligence (AI) – the simulation of human intelligence by a machine

Automatic – the ability of a machine to perform a task without input from a human

Autonomous – the ability of a computer to perform a task without input from a human, but including the ability to react to circumstances as it finds them

Barcode – a series of stripes that contain data and can be scanned by a barcode reader device

Digital technology – any device or system that creates, stores or uses data

Event-driven programming – a style of programming where all code is written to respond to events, for example when a button is pressed

Fail – the expected outcome of the test does not happen

Invalid data – data that should *not* be accepted by a program

Pass – the expected outcome of the test happens when the test is performed

Radio Frequency Identification (RFID) tag – this contains data that can be read via a radio signal when the tag is close to a reader

Radio signal – a signal within a specific frequency band, used to transmit data

Trigger – cause to happen

Valid data – data that should be accepted by a program

Reflect: What can you do now that you couldn't do before?

Glossary of key terms

Advertisement – a notice telling people about a product

AI image generator – a piece of software that uses artificial intelligence to generate images based on a text description typed in by the user

Application software – allows the computer user to do a task, for example a web browser or a word processor

Artificial intelligence (AI) – the simulation of human intelligence by a machine

ASCII – American Standard Code for Information Interchange, a commonly used format for encoding characters on a computer

Audience – the people who will look at the work you produce

Augmented reality – using technology to superimpose digital content on top of a real-world environment

Automatic – the ability of a machine to perform a task without input from a human

Autonomous – the ability of a computer to perform a task without input from a human, but including the ability to react to circumstances as it finds them

Barcode – a series of stripes that contain data and can be scanned by a barcode reader device

Big Data – an extremely large amount of data, which might be used to train a machine learning model

Binary – a number system which represents numbers using only two values: 0 and 1

Bit – a single **b**inary dig**it**, either 0 or 1

Boolean – a type of data that can have one of two possible values: true or false

Cast – change the data type of a piece of data

Character – any single letter, number, space or punctuation mark

Checkbox – a form input that allows one or more choices to be made from a list of options

Code review – a software developer checking code written by another developer and suggesting improvements

Comment – a note written for a human to read in a program. All comments are completely ignored by the computer

Comparison operator – an operator that allows you to compare two values, for example to check whether they are equal, or one is greater than the other

Compression – significantly reducing the amount of storage space a file requires

Concatenation – joining two or more pieces of text together

Condition – a test in a program that evaluates to a Boolean value – either true or false

Constant – a value that does not change while the program is running

Cookie – a small amount of data stored on your computer by a website

Copper cable – a type of cable which uses copper wire to transmit an electrical signal

Data mining – analysing large amounts of data to find patterns and trends

Database – an organised collection of data, usually stored on a computer

Decomposition – the process of breaking down a complex problem into smaller, more manageable tasks

Denary – the familiar base-10 number system which uses the digits 0–9

Digital technology – any device or system that creates, stores or uses data

Driver – a small piece of software that allows the operating system to communicate with a hardware device such as a printer

Dry run – simulate how an algorithm will run by tracing how the value of each variable changes

Echo check – a test to see whether data has been transmitted correctly, which repeats the data back to the sender and checks for differences

Emoji – a small icon used in text to express an emotion or represent an item

Ethernet cable – a type of network cable used to connect computers and other network devices such as routers together

Event-driven programming – a style of programming where all code is written to respond to events, for example when a button is pressed

Fail – the expected outcome of the test does not happen

Fibre optic cable – a type of cable which uses flexible glass fibres to transmit data as pulses of light

File access permissions – restrict access to files and folders on a network to only the people who need to see them

Firewall – provides a layer of protection between two networks, preventing threats from entering, and sensitive information from leaving

Flow of control – the order in which the statements in a program are executed

Form – a method of collecting specific data, often to be added to a database

GIF – an image format that allows animation

Hotspot – an area on the screen that the user can click on to perform an action

Indentation – positioning code further in from the left

Instant message – a short text-based message which is delivered immediately, allowing them to be used for a real-time conversation

Interference – disruption or alteration to an electrical signal

Internet of Things (IoT) – a network of interconnected devices, appliances and physical objects, typically containing sensors, which communicate across the internet

Invalid data – data that should *not* be accepted by a program

IP address – an address allocated to you by your internet service provider, which reveals your rough geographical location. An IP address looks like a set of four numbers separated with a dot, for example 172.217.22.14

Iterative development – regularly adding new features and improvements to a piece of software, and then seeking feedback to inform the next set of improvements

LAN – Local Area Network, a network which connects devices in one physical location, for example a school or an office

Length check – checks that the length of the data typed in is within a range

Linear search – an algorithm that checks each item in a list in turn until the search item is found, or the end of the list is reached

List – a data structure that can hold more than one piece of data

Live stream – to broadcast an online event as it happens, for example someone playing a video game, or presenting to the camera

Logic gate – a circuit inside a computer that allows Boolean logic to be applied to one or more inputs

Logical operator – AND, OR or NOT

Machine learning – an area of computer science that uses algorithms and data to create software that can improve its own performance

Malware – **mali**cious soft**ware**. Any software that intends to cause harm to a computer, for example a virus

Meme – a familiar image, often accompanied with text, which is shared and reused on the internet

Metadata – 'data about data', for example who created the data, when it was created, and what device it was created on.

Model – a simulation of a real-life system on a computer

Multimedia – using more than one method of presenting information, e.g. text, images, sound and/or video

Navigation – the way a user moves through a presentation or a website

Network – a collection of computers that are connected together to exchange data

Operating system (OS) – an important piece of software which manages all other software and hardware devices

Packet – a chunk of data being transmitted across a network, e.g. the internet

PAN – Personal Area Network, a network which connects the devices within range of one person

Pass – the expected outcome of the test happens when the test is performed

Place value – the value that a digit has because of its position ('place') in the number

Port – a number assigned to each type of network traffic going in or out of a firewall

Presence check – checks whether a form field has been filled in

Primary key – an assigned field in a database table that contains data that is both unique and not empty for every record

Program library – a collection of pre-written code that can be imported and used within another program

Program logic – how the design of the program is implemented

Pseudocode – a method of planning a program using statements that have a clear and precise meaning, but are not written in any particular programming language

Radio button – a form input that allows a single choice to be made from a list of options

Radio Frequency Identification (RFID) tag – contains data that can be read via a radio signal when the tag is close to a reader

Radio signal – a signal within a specific frequency band, used to transmit data

RAM – Random Access Memory, used to store instructions and data the computer is currently working with. Contents are lost when the power is switched off

Random – chosen by chance

Record – a piece of information written down in a permanent form, to be used for later reference

ROM – Read Only Memory, stores the instructions needed to load the operating system. Contents are kept when the power is switched off

Router – a networking device that connects two or more networks together

Run length encoding (RLE) – a compression method which allows files with repeating patterns to potentially be stored more efficiently

Scheduling – a task performed by the operating system to make sure each piece of software gets a turn to use the processor

Search term – the text you write into a search engine to find what you need

Searching algorithm – a method of finding a specific item in a list.

Selection – when a program executes different code based on a condition

Sequence – statements in code that execute in the order they are written

Social media – a website or an app which allows users to share text, image and video content with others they are connected to

String – a sequence of letters, numbers and/or punctuation, usually written within quotation marks

Syntax – the structure of a statement in a programming language

Table – a collection of related data, stored as columns and rows

Template – a pre-designed format for a document

Text box – a form input that accepts string data

Text-based programming language – allows you to type text instructions that a computer can run

Trace table – records how the values of variables in an algorithm change as the steps of the algorithm are followed

Training – providing data to a machine learning algorithm so that it can recognise patterns in the data

Transmission error – a problem which occurs when data is sent across a network

Transmit – send a signal from one place to another

Trigger – cause to happen

Troubleshooter – a tool that gathers information to pinpoint the cause of a problem, and then offers advice on how to fix it

Truth table – a diagram showing all possible combinations of inputs and outputs from a Boolean expression

Type check – checks that the data entered has the correct data type

Unicode – a character encoding format which can encode characters in any language

Uniform Resource Locator (URL) – a unique address which specifies the location of a website

User feedback – feedback from a person who uses a piece of software

Utility software – keeps the computer secure and in working order, for example antivirus software

Valid data – data that should be accepted by a program

Validation – data typed into a form is checked to see whether it is a sensible value

Virtual tour – a simulation of being at a particular location, involving multimedia such as images, text and perhaps also sound and video

Voice chat – a method of online communication via speech, often involving joining a channel with a specified theme

WAN – Wide Area Network, a network which connects devices over a large geographical

'What if' scenario – a simulation involving a set of criteria being applied to a model, so that the result can be observed

Wired network – computers and network devices connected using physical cables such as ethernet cables

Wireless network – computers and network devices that connect and communicate via radio signals

Acknowledgements

Screenshots

Support materials and screenshots are licensed under the Creative Commons Attribution-ShareAlike 2.0 license. We are grateful to the following for permission to reproduce screenshots. In some instances, we have been unable to trace the owners of copyright material, and we would appreciate any information that would enable us to do so.

Python Software Foundation: permission obtained to use screenshots demonstrating Python programming language features.

Scratch Foundation: authorised usage of screenshots showcasing Scratch programming environment elements.

Machine Learning for Kids: kindly granted permission for the incorporation of screenshots illustrating machine learning concepts and tools designed for educational purposes.

EduBlocks: Granted clearance for the inclusion of screenshots depicting EduBlocks interface and functionalities.

Scratch is developed by the Lifelong Kindergarten Group at the MIT Media Lab: p.40–42, p.45, p.90, p.140.

PSF's License Agreement and PSF's notice of copyright, i.e., "Copyright (c) 2001 Python Software Foundation; All Rights Reserved" are retained in Python 2.0.1 alone or in any derivative version prepared by Collins (Licensee): p.39–45, p.49, p.52–54, p.79, p.82, p.84–86, p.89–91, p.93, p.144–145.

EduBlocks: p.40–42, p.84, p.133, p.140–142.

Images

We are grateful for the following for permission to reproduce their images:

p.3 Oleksiy Mark/Shutterstock, p.4 adichrisworo/Shutterstock, p.5 Stokkete/Shutterstock, p.5 ViDI Studio/Shutterstock, p.5 Vladimir Sukhachev/Shutterstock, p.5 William Potter/Shutterstock, p.7 McLittle Stock/Shutterstock, p.7 DC Studio/Shutterstock, p.8 selinofoto/Shutterstock, p.8 NicoElNino/Shutterstock, p.11 metamorworks/Shutterstock, p.12 Shishir Gautam/Shutterstock, p.13 leungchopan/Shutterstock, p.14 Artem Shevchenko/Shutterstock, p.21 gpointstudio/Shutterstock, p.21 StevenWilcox/Shutterstock, p.21 Panther Media GmbH/Shutterstock, p.22 New Africa/Shutterstock, p.23 panuwat phimpha/Shutterstock, p.23 stas11/Shutterstock, p.24 Ian Dyball/Shutterstock, p.24 Sudowoodo/Shutterstock, p.25 Graphic farm/Shutterstock, p.26 Vectorsh/Shutterstock, p.31 UfaBizPhoto/Shutterstock, p.31 Structured Vision/Shutterstock, p.31 metamorworks/Shutterstock, p.31 Gatot Adri/Shutterstock, p.32 Boris Stroujko/Shutterstock, p.32 reddees/Shutterstock, p.35 Antonio Guillem/Shutterstock, p.36 yut_art/Shutterstock, p.36 Prostock-studio/Shutterstock, p.37 Zapp2Photo/Shutterstock, p.37 Andrey_Popov/Shutterstock, p.44 Vector Tradition/Shutterstock, p.46 GoodStudio/Shutterstock, p.46 Elena Pimukova/Shutterstock, p.48 Gorynvd/Shutterstock, p.48 Laboo Studio/Shutterstock, p.48 ebonyeg/Shutterstock, p.49 NotionPic/Shutterstock, p.51 Mihai_Andritoiu/Shutterstock, p.53 ne2pi/Shutterstock, p.55 SeventyFour/Shutterstock, p.56 Elena Schweitzer/Shutterstock, p.60 luchschenF/Shutterstock, p.60 Levent Konuk/Shutterstock, p.63 klyaksun/Shutterstock, p.64 hanss/Shutterstock, p.66 klyaksun/Shutterstock, p.66 JMiks/Shutterstock, p.67 Jarretera/Shutterstock, p.71 Antonio Guillem/Shutterstock, p.72 Dragon Claws/Shutterstock, p.73 Maxx-Studio/Shutterstock, p.73 BritCats Studio/Shutterstock, p.74 r.classen/Shutterstock, p.74 RightFramePhotoVideo/Shutterstock, p.74 Dragon Images/Shutterstock, p.74 Andrey_Popov/Shutterstock, p.102 Flegere/Shutterstock, p.102 VectorManZone/Shutterstock, p.103 metamorworks/Shutterstock, p.105 ST.art/Shutterstock, p.107 Tero Vesalainen/Shutterstock, p.107 Gorodenkoff/Shutterstock, p.108 fizkes/Shutterstock, p.108 Tirachard Kumtanom/Shutterstock, p.108 Gorodenkoff/Shutterstock, p.109 NicoElNino/Shutterstock, p.110 dubassy/Shutterstock, p.117 Volha Valadzionak/Shutterstock, p.117 Public domain, p.117 Public domain, p.125 connel/Shutterstock, p.128 GoodStudio/Shutterstock, p.130 nimito/Shutterstock, p.131 Ye Liew/Shutterstock, p.134 brizmaker/Shutterstock, p.134 panuwat phimpha/Shutterstock, p.135 Gorodenkoff/Shutterstock, p.135 IM Imagery/Shutterstock, p.135 frantic00/Shutterstock, p.136 metamorworks/Shutterstock, p.136 WINDCOLORS/Shutterstock, p.137 Baloncici/Shutterstock, p.137 Summit Art Creations/Shutterstock, p.138 Ira Lichi/Shutterstock, p.139 Volkova/Shutterstock, p.140 Theodoros Kitsos/Shutterstock, p.149 RATTAR/Shutterstock.